STRE

For Tough Times

STRENGTH
FOR TOUGH TIMES

MARIA KNEAS

EXPANDED 2ND EDITION

LIGHTHOUSE TRAILS PUBLISHING
EUREKA, MONTANA

Strength for Tough Times
©2010, 2016 by Maria Kneas
Expanded 2nd Edition 2016

Lighthouse Trails Publishing, LLC
P.O. Box 908
Eureka, MT 59917
www.lighthousetrails.com

Library of Congress Cataloging-in-Publication Data

Names: Kneas, Maria M., author.
Title: Strength for tough times : encouragement from God's word / Maria M.
   Kneas.
Description: Expanded 2nd Edition. | Eureka : Lighthouse Trails Publishing,
   2016. | Includes bibliographical references.
Identifiers: LCCN 2016027715 | ISBN 9781942423102 (softbound : alk. paper)
Subjects: LCSH: Trust in God--Christianity. | Christian life.
Classification: LCC BV4637 .K56 2016 | DDC 248.8/6--dc23 LC record available at https://lccn.loc.gov/2016027715.

Printed in the United States of America

To my husband, Ray,
who went home to be with the Lord
and is in a much better place
than we are.

The rest of us still face trials
in "this present evil world."
(Galatians 1:4)

But God is faithful—
His love is beyond our comprehension,
His grace is sufficient for all our needs,
and His Word gives us comfort
and guidance.

CONTENTS

THESE THINGS I HAVE
SPOKEN UNTO YOU,
THAT IN ME YE MIGHT HAVE PEACE.
IN THE WORLD YE SHALL
HAVE TRIBULATION:
BUT BE OF GOOD CHEER;
I HAVE OVERCOME THE WORLD.
(JOHN 16:33)

PREFACE

SURPRISING events have been happening in America, and many things we used to trust no longer seem to be reliable. How can we find security, peace, and joy under such circumstances?

Only God has enough love, power, and faithfulness to be our defense, our rescuer, and our refuge. He is the solid Rock on which we can safely stand (Psalm 62:5-7). Everything else is only "sinking sand," promising safety for a while, but sooner or later utterly failing.

How can we apply these Scriptural principles to everyday life? *Strength for Tough Times* has practical lessons I learned the hard way—in the furnace of affliction. That is where we discover how much we can trust God.

I know something about affliction because I watched my husband die. And I can testify that God is faithful. He loves us, and He will bring good out of everything that happens to us if we love Him (Romans 8:28).

Never be afraid to trust
an unknown future
to a known God.

(Corrie ten Boom)

CHAPTER 1

A RUDE AWAKENING

Awake thou that sleepest, and arise from the dead, and
Christ shall give thee light. (Ephesians 5:14)

BACK in 2006, I had major surgery. I woke up in the Intensive
Care Unit on a respirator with my hands tied to the railings of
the hospital bed.

It would have been easy for me to panic in that situation, but
God gave me the grace to pray instead. I said, "God, show me how
to live in this place." And He did.

I noticed a device on one of my fingers that kept track of the
oxygen level. I rubbed that finger against the railing and was able
to inch the thing off. That set off an alarm, and a nurse came into
the room to see what was wrong.

I waved at her with both hands in order to get her attention, and
she started watching me. Then I held one hand up straight like a pad
of paper, and with the other hand, I made motions like I was writing with a pen. So she asked me if I wanted a pen and some paper,

and I nodded "yes." She gave them to me, and I wrote questions, which she answered. And from then on, we could communicate.

I saw my inital writing days later that at first was all over the paper because of my high dose of morphine. Once the nurse saw I wouldn't try to pull the tubes out of my nose, she decreased the morphine and loosened the ropes that were tying my hands. That way, I could write more easily, and we could communicate better. In addition, we could work as a team. They regularly siphoned fluid out of my lungs. I learned how to tell when there was fluid in them, so I developed hand motions to let the nurse know. She then would listen to my lungs and remove the fluid.

My stay in the hospital was only temporary, but something similar has happened when it comes to living here in America. Unfortunately, this is not short term at all, and it seems to be getting worse and worse—sliding downhill faster and faster. The United States has become a strange, unexpected place, and we need to have God show us how to live here. Things are getting surreal.

Do you remember when Americans loved to watch *Leave it to Beaver, The Waltons*, and *Little House on the Prairie*? How did this nation morph into a place where people enjoy watching *Wicked City* (which is about two serial killers, showing very graphic sex and very gory violence) and *Lucifer* (which features the devil as a handsome, charming good guy who has left Hell and now runs a nightclub in Los Angeles)? These shows are on mainstream channels (ABC and Fox), and they can be watched by impressionable children all over the United States. *Wicked City* aired beginning in October 2015, and *Lucifer* had thirteen episodes starting on January 25, 2016. *Lucifer* did so well that it will be back again starting on September 19, 2016.

Where did America go? What strange country are we living in now? And how can we live in a place like this and still be faithful Christians in spite of the rampant corruption? We need to pray, "Lord show us how to live *in* the world but not *of* the world." Jesus conveyed this idea when He prayed to the Father:

I have given them thy word; and the world hath hated them, because they are not of the world, even as I am not of the world. I pray not that thou shouldest take them out of the world, but that thou shouldest keep them from the evil. *They are not of the world*, even as I am not of the world. Sanctify them through thy truth: thy word is truth. As thou hast sent me into the world, even so have *I also sent them into the world.* (John 17:14-18)

The Bible tells us how we can live in this world even though we are not of it. It worked for the early church, the Christians who lived in ancient Rome, which was incredibly corrupt and depraved. Therefore, it will also work for us now as we live in postmodern America.

The Bible tells us about God, and His ways, and His amazing love for us. It tells us how to live and what is waiting for those who abide in Him (1 John 2:28).

No matter what happens to us down here on planet Earth, the most important thing is to spend eternity with Him in Heaven and to help others get there too. Look at what we have waiting for us:

They shall hunger no more, neither thirst any more; neither shall the sun light on them, nor any heat. For the Lamb which is in the midst of the throne shall feed them, and shall lead them unto living fountains of waters: and God shall wipe away all tears from their eyes. (Revelation 7:16-17)

Worthy is the Lamb that was slain to receive power, and riches, and wisdom, and strength, and honour, and glory, and blessing. (Revelation 5:12)

HE GIVETH MORE GRACE
by Annie Johnson Flint (1866-1932)

He giveth more grace
as our burdens grow greater.
He sendeth more strength
as our labors increase;
To added afflictions,
He addeth His mercy.
To multiplied trials,
He multiplies peace.

When we have exhausted
our store of endurance,
When our strength has failed
Ere the day is half done,
When we reach the end
Of our hoarded resources,
Our Father's full giving is only begun.

His love has no limits,
His grace has no measure,
His power no boundary known unto men;
For out of His infinite riches in Jesus
He giveth, and giveth, and giveth again.

CHAPTER 2

HELPING BROKEN HEARTS

He healeth the broken in heart, and bindeth up their wounds. (Psalm 147:3)

WHEN my husband Ray died, I was devastated. We had been very close, and my life was shattered by his death. I often cried myself to sleep at night.

Then one day, I realized something. Once your heart has been broken, it will never be the same again. Either you can turn inward on yourself, or you can open outwardly and love more people in more ways than before. So I made a deliberate decision to open my heart and look for people who need help and love.

I found an old lady in my apartment building who needed practical help and companionship. I also tried to help our resident manager; people only spoke to her when they had complaints or problems, so I made a point of stopping by to encourage her. There were also some homeless people on the street in front of our apartment building, so I made sandwiches for them. And eventually I wound up being a live-in housemother for mentally handicapped adults.

Of course, doing that didn't get rid of the heartache. It's been over 38 years, and I still miss Ray so much that if I see somebody who reminds me of him, I break down crying. However, my days are focused on other things. They are filled with helping and loving people and reaching out to them.

If I had turned inward on myself, my days would have been filled with self-pity, and I would have wound up with my heart becoming harder. But because I made a decision to reach out to others instead, God has made my heart more tender and more loving toward both God and other people.

There is also another principle involving being brokenhearted. In the Sermon on the Mount, Jesus told us:

> Blessed are they that mourn: for they shall be comforted. (Matthew 5:4)

I realize it sure doesn't feel like a blessing at the time. But remember Romans 8:28:

> And we know that all things work together for good to them that love God, to them who are the called according to his purpose.

Something happened in my life that is a small illustration of these two Scriptures. When I was about eighteen, I was smitten with an older man named Pierre. He was a perfect gentleman who treated me like a princess and never tried to get fresh with me. Pierre worked for the State Department. We met because we both studied classical guitar with the same teacher.

Back then, I lived in Washington, DC. One day Pierre and I were walking together in Georgetown in an area that had cobblestones. I was wearing spike heel shoes. Well, spike heels and cobblestones are not a good combination. It's too easy to step down on a cobblestone in the wrong way and sprain your ankle, and that is precisely what happened to me. One minute we were cheerfully walking along together, and the next minute I was hobbling in pain.

Pierre immediately put his strong arm around my shoulders to help support me so I could walk. And from then on, his arm was around me until I got back home.

Now that ankle still hurt, but it was so wonderful having Pierre's arm around me that I didn't care about the pain. I was actually grateful for that sprained ankle because it resulted in him holding me close.

That is a very small and inadequate picture of how wonderful it will be when God wipes away our tears in Heaven. It will be so tender and so precious and so beautiful that we will be grateful we had tears that needed to be wiped away.

Like that sprained ankle, temporary pain will turn into tremendous blessing while we, with grateful hearts that once were broken, find God's comfort as He wipes our tears away. Yes, it will be so incredibly wonderful.

> For the Lamb which is in the midst of the throne shall feed them, and shall lead them unto living fountains of waters: and God shall wipe away all tears from their eyes. (Revelation 7:17)

> But as it is written, Eye hath not seen, nor ear heard, neither have entered into the heart of man, the things which God hath prepared for them that love him. (1 Corinthians 2:9)

ONLY TO LOVE AND SERVE THEE

Thy voice I hear, Lord Jesus,
Bidding me walk with Thee,—
Carry the cross Thou givest,
Rough tho' the path may be.
Often I've dreaded leaving
All for Thyself alone,
Hoping I still might please Thee,
Now I'd be all Thine own.

The world's vain fleeting follies
Have kept from liberty,
Now I renounce each idol
That I loved more than Thee.
Henceforth to serve Thee only
All my life I would spend,
Knowing Thy grace unfailing
Will keep me to the end.

With Thee I'd walk, my Saviour—
Following day by day,
Tho' it mean trial and hardship,
Sacrifice all the way,—
For Thou hast grace sufficient,
With Thee I will not fear.
Heaven would lose its sweetness
If all were easy here.

Refrain:
Only to love and serve Thee
Daily to bear the cross,
Counting for Thee, my Saviour,
Treasures of earth as dross.

CHAPTER 3

BE CAUTIOUS AND ALERT

See then that ye walk circumspectly, not as fools, but as wise, Redeeming the time, because the days are evil. (Ephesians 5:15-16)

RECENTLY, I had lunch at a local restaurant, and I noticed that a woman in the booth next to mine was wearing a tee-shirt that said, "Proud To Be A Hater." I asked her what that meant, and she said she was a Cowboys fan, and therefore she hated the Redskins. Seeing that shirt shocked me. "Proud to be a hater" is the kind of thing I would expect to hear from an ISIS terrorist—not from a middle-aged American woman who chatted pleasantly with me after I asked her about her shirt.

Suppose that two men whose fathers are professional football players are serving together in Afghanistan. The father of one man plays for the Cowboys and the father of the other man plays for the Redskins. Would they hate one another? I don't think so. They would be too busy protecting one another's backs against a common enemy.

If the Cowboys and the Redskins played against one another in the Superbowl, would they care if their father's team won? Of course they would. But for men who have seen fellow soldiers blown up by bombs or shot down by enemies, the Superbowl would not be foremost in their minds. The safety of their buddies would be far more important to them. When you are at war, then your perspective about things changes significantly.

According to the Bible, every Christian is in a *spiritual* war. Our enemies are the world system, the flesh, and the devil. Therefore, we need to be vigilant and careful about what we do because small mistakes can have large consequences.

You can see that principle even in ordinary everyday activities like driving our cars. If we make a left turn at the wrong time due to carelessness, then we will get broadsided by another vehicle. That would cost us time, money, and a lot of hassle; and it could result in life-changing injuries or even death. During war time, the degree of risk and potential damage becomes much greater.

According to *Webster's Dictionary*, *circumspect* means "careful to consider all circumstances and possible consequences; prudent." A synonym is *cautious*, and in defining that, the dictionary explains some differences in words related to circumspect. It says, "Cautious implies the exercise of forethought usually prompted by fear of probable or even of merely possible danger; circumspect suggests less fear and stresses the surveying of all possible consequences before acting or deciding; *wary* emphasizes suspiciousness and alertness in watching for danger and cunning in escaping it."

We are living in a world that has rejected Christ and is going crazy. Therefore, if we want to be faithful Christians, we need to be cautious, circumspect, and wary. All of these different attributes are important if we want to protect our relationship with God and with other believers.

We need to be aware of what we are thinking and feeling. Not everything we think and feel comes from us. Sometimes it can be from the Holy Spirit, and sometimes it can be from demons.

We also need to be aware of *what* is influencing us and *how* it is influencing us. We can ask God to give us an "early warning system" that sets off red alarm lights when something is influencing us in a bad way.

Above all, we need to know the Bible for ourselves and not depend on getting information about it secondhand (from sermons and books, etc.); and we need to have a prayer life. We need to keep a solid connection between ourselves and the Lord.

When my husband Ray was alive, he and I could be in the same room, intensely focused on different things and not talking to one another. But even though we were not communicating verbally or looking at one another, we were very much aware of the presence of our "other half." There was always a level of connection between us. And, of course, we would talk from time to time, and there were times when we were intensely focused on one another.

After Ray died, it was amazing how empty our home felt. While he was alive, if I was in one room by myself and he was somewhere else, I still didn't feel alone. But after Ray died, the aloneness was overwhelming.

I'm in my 70s now, and I've been reading the Bible, thinking about what it says, and talking with the Lord for a long time. I always feel His presence, like I used to feel my husband's presence. That connection is always there.

Some things can interfere with that. One time, I was watching one of the old Star Trek movies with my nephews, and I felt that connection go away. Well, I used to be a Trekkie when the old series first came out, so that show grabbed me in a way that most TV shows don't. After that experience, I never watched Star Trek again, and I radically decreased all TV.

Now, I'm not saying that everybody should do that. People are all different. But we do need to be aware of what is going on and the impact that things are having on us.

For me, having that ongoing connection with the Lord is far more important than any form of entertainment. I enjoy good entertainment, but I can live without it. However, I cannot live without being in communion with the Lord. I constantly need His guidance, His comfort, and His encouragement.

If America becomes a more dangerous place, then that will become true for many more people. For example, if we could run into an ISIS terrorist at any street corner, then all of a sudden, prayer would become much more important to us. Who cares about the latest movie or football game when you don't know whether or not you will be able to get home without having your head get cut off by some terrorist? Plus, you want to be sure that your spouse and your children made it home safely. And you want to know that your friends are all right. Under those kinds of circumstances, all at once our priorities change radically.

Quite apart from terrorists, being *tuned in* to God has important practical consequences. One time, I was at the base of one of those high, curved bridges where you can't see what's on the other side of the bridge. I was waiting for the light to tell me I could make a left-hand turn. The light changed, and I was about to make that turn. Then I had a strong feeling that I needed to freeze and stay right where I was. I didn't "hear" anything or know that it was God communicating with me. But I had this strong feeling, and I followed it. I didn't move. And then a truck came barreling over the bridge. Evidently, he had run the red light on the other side of the bridge.

If I had made that turn when the light told me to do it, I would have been broadsided by that truck. So even when things seem to be safe and normal, it is still good to be tuned in to the Lord as much as possible. We can just be aware of Him and receptive to any way He wants to nudge us or guide us.

With me, it's much similar to how it was with my husband. Sometimes I focus intensely on God. I frequently chat with Him (thanking Him for His blessings, asking for His help or guidance, etc.). And I'm always aware of His presence. I never feel alone.

I'm nobody special. If God does that for me, then He can do it for anyone who will receive Him. Isaiah said, "every one that thirsteth come ye to the waters" (Isaiah 55:1). Jesus was and is the water of life, and He promised the gift of the Holy Spirit to those who will receive Him (John 4:14).

CHAPTER 4

TRUSTING GOD

PROVERBS 3:5-8 gives some keys to having a right relationship with God. It also shows us how God will bless us if we do things His way.

Frank Sinatra used to sing a song called "My Way." Its theme is, "I did it my way." This is a good example of leaning on your own understanding and being wise in your own eyes—which is a recipe for disaster.

Here is what God tells us in Proverbs 3:5-8. (I give each verse separately so we can look at them individually.)

> Trust in the LORD with all thine heart; and lean not unto thine own understanding. (vs. 5)

> In all thy ways acknowledge him, and he shall direct thy paths. (vs. 6)

> Be not wise in thine own eyes: fear the LORD, and depart from evil. (vs. 7)

It shall be health to thy navel, and marrow to thy bones. (vs. 8)

Verse 5 gives a contrast between two opposing things. Trusting in the Lord with all your heart is comparable to a child who is walking with his father, and they have their arms around each other. That child is not going to go in the wrong direction or the wrong way. And he is not going to fall. He is safe and secure. If the ground is uneven or unstable, the father will support the child, and he will guide him onto safe paths.

According to *Strong's Concordance*, the word "lean" means to lean on or rely on. Leaning on our own understanding means to rely on our own intellect, training, and experience more than we rely on God. We need to use those things (which are gifts from God), but our primary reliance should be on God Himself. Our human understanding is so limited. Our human experience is so inadequate compared to that of the Creator of the universe. We only see "in a mirror, dimly" (1 Corinthians 13:12). Our vision is clouded. Our perspective is too narrow. God tells us:

> For my thoughts are not your thoughts, neither are your ways my ways, saith the LORD. For as the heavens are higher than the earth, so are my ways higher than your ways, and my thoughts than your thoughts. (Isaiah 55:8-9)

Even if things happen that we don't understand, we can trust God's nature, character, power, and love. The apostle Paul said:

> For the which cause I also suffer these things: nevertheless I am not ashamed: for I know whom I have believed, and am persuaded that he is able to keep that which I have committed unto him against that day. (2 Timothy 1:12)

Notice that Paul said whom (a person) rather than what (a thing). Paul's confidence was in God rather than in his own understanding.

Leaning on our own understanding is comparable to walking with a cane and putting most of our weight on it. If the cane lands on uneven ground (such as a rocky place) or at an awkward angle (as it could in a hole or in a crack between some rocks), then we can stumble. If it lands on unstable ground (such as stones that move or a slippery surface), then we can fall. The cane doesn't know which way is safe and which way is dangerous. It just goes where we put it. And it can only provide stability to the degree we have chosen solid footing for it.

According to *Strong's Concordance*, the word "acknowledge" in Proverbs 3:6 includes comprehending, considering, being diligent, receiving instruction, being aware, having respect, understanding, being acquainted with, and being related to (as a kinsman). It involves the kind of understanding that comes from personal relationship in addition to diligently paying attention to (and comprehending) instruction. When we have a close personal relationship with the Lord and pay close attention to what He tells us and shows us, then He will direct our paths.

God stores what we have read in our hearts and minds as in a treasury. Then, as we face each day, His Holy Spirit quickens His Word to us, which becomes "a lamp unto my feet, and a light unto my path" (Psalm 119:105).

Proverbs 3:7 gives a contrast between two things: The first is being wise in our own eyes, and the second is fearing the Lord and departing from evil. If we are wise in our own eyes, then it is difficult to have a biblical fear of the Lord.

In addition, being wise in our own eyes can lead to sins such as presumption, doubt, unbelief, pride, and hardness of heart. Examples of such sins are given in the following Scripture passages:

Keep back thy servant also from presumptuous sins; let them not have dominion over me: then shall I be upright, and I shall be innocent from the great transgression. (Psalm 19:13)

Take heed, brethren, lest there be in any of you an evil heart of unbelief, in departing from the living God. (Hebrews 3:12)

Afterward he [Jesus] appeared unto the eleven as they sat at meat, and upbraided them with their unbelief and hardness of heart, because they believed not them which had seen him after he was risen. (Mark 16:14)

Following the guidelines of Proverbs 3:5-7 will bring blessings in our lives. Verse 8 says, "It shall be health to thy navel, and marrow to thy bones."

When we lean on our own understanding instead of fully trusting the Lord, we can become stressed or anxious. According to medical research, sustained stress can cause arthritis and anemia, which are diseases of the bones and bone marrow. (The bone marrow makes the blood.) Stress can also cause, or aggravate, other health problems.

Verse 8 mentions health for our "navel." According to *Strong's Concordance*, the Hebrew word used here literally means the umbilical cord. How does a baby in the womb get everything he needs for life? Through the umbilical cord. If it doesn't function properly, then the baby won't get adequate food and oxygen.

A baby in the womb is totally dependent upon his mother for everything he needs for life. He is connected to his mother by the umbilical cord, and he receives what he needs through that cord. Similarly, the Christian is totally dependent upon God for everything. Receiving what God wants to give us depends on our being rightly connected to Him.

Whatever we need, in order to receive it, we have to be rightly related to God. Do we need strength or comfort or courage or healing or wisdom or protection or provision? Remember, Proverbs 3:5-8 gives us some keys for receiving such things from God.

Building Trust

How can we develop the child-like faith of trusting in the Lord with all of our heart instead of leaning on our own understanding? There are some practical things we can do to help strengthen our trust in God.

Strengthening Our Relationship

When you know a good person intimately—when you really know that person's heart—then you have more trust in him or her. So how do we get to know God better? By reading the Bible and asking God to help us understand it. The Bible shows us God's character and His ways.

We can also get to know God better by spending time in prayer and worship. The Bible says:

> Be careful [anxious] for nothing; but in every thing by prayer and supplication with thanksgiving let your requests be made known unto God. And the peace of God, which passeth all understanding, shall keep your hearts and minds through Christ Jesus. (Philippians 4:6-7)

Notice that the peace comes when we give things to God in prayer. It does not wait for how He answers our prayers. It does not depend on the outcome. The peace comes when we put the situation into God's hands. The Bible says we should cast all our cares (concerns) on God because He loves and takes care of us (1 Peter 5:7).

Gratitude

We need to develop the habit of being grateful for who God is and what He has already done for us. It is easy to take things for granted. For example, you are reading this book. Have you thanked God for the fact that you are able to see, and you know how to read?

27

If we look for things to thank God for, we will find more and more reasons to be grateful. And if we look for things to complain about, we will find more and more reasons to complain.

When the Israelites came out of Egypt and went to the Promised Land, they kept complaining. They got bored with eating manna every day and wanted to eat something more flavorful (with garlic and leeks). So they complained about the miraculous food God provided. They complained when they had no water. God miraculously supplied water for them, but we have no record they were grateful for it.

And what was the end of the matter? That generation died in the wilderness because they refused to enter the Promised Land when God told them to. They didn't trust God to deal with the giants there.

This is an example of how a lack of gratitude can result in a lack of trusting God. And that can lead to a lack of obedience (i.e., rebellion against God).

THE LORD IS MY ROCK, AND MY FORTRESS, AND MY DELIVERER; MY GOD, MY STRENGTH, IN WHOM I WILL TRUST. (PSALM 18:2)

Compare this with the attitude of King Jehoshaphat. When he and his people were threatened by a huge army, Jehoshaphat prayed:

> O our God, wilt thou not judge them? for we have no might against this great company that cometh against us; neither know we what to do: but *our eyes are upon thee.* (2 Chronicles 20:12, emphasis added)

And God came through for them. He miraculously delivered them from their enemies.

We can choose to develop the habit of thanking God. We can look for things to thank Him for. We can thank God and praise Him even when we don't feel like it.

We can deliberately choose to be grateful, and we can ask God to give us a grateful heart. The apostle Paul exhorted us to have that kind of attitude when he said:

> *Rejoice evermore. Pray without ceasing. In every thing give thanks:* for this is the will of God in Christ Jesus concerning you. (1 Thessalonians 5:16-18, emphasis added)

Corrie ten Boom and her sister Betsy were sent to a Nazi concentration camp because their family hid Jews during World War II. Betsy died in that camp, but Corrie was released.[1] After the war, Corrie traveled the world, telling people about God's love. She knew first-hand how difficult life can be, when she said:

Never be afraid to trust an unknown future to a known God.[2]

Betsy ten Boom was able to love the Nazis and pray for their salvation even while surrounded by the horrors of a death camp. In spite of the horrible things the prison guards did to the prisoners, she saw them as being trapped and tormented. She saw their need for God's love and forgiveness. She prayed for their salvation, and by her example, she led other prisoners to do the same.

Betsy reminds me of Stephen, who was the first Christian martyr. While he was being stoned by an angry mob, he prayed for his persecutors:

> And he kneeled down, and cried with a loud voice, Lord, lay not this sin to their charge. And when he had said this, he fell asleep. (Acts 7:60)

At first, Corrie hated the Nazis, but eventually she was able to forgive them. After the war, she heard that Jan Vogel, the man who had betrayed her family, was in prison and was to be executed. She wrote to him, telling him she forgave him and telling him about the love of Jesus Christ. Shortly before he was executed, Jan Vogel wrote back to Corrie, telling her he had become a Christian.

When Corrie was ministering in Germany, a man came up to her after the service. He had been a prison guard in Ravensbruck, the death camp where Betsy died. He held out his hand to Corrie, asking if she forgave him. At first, Corrie was overwhelmed by memories from the prison camp, and she froze. Then she asked God to help her love this man. She forced herself to put out her hand to take his. When they held hands, God's love flooded Corrie's heart, and she and her former tormentor embraced one another as fellow children of God.

> And hope maketh not ashamed; because the love of God is shed abroad in our hearts by the Holy Ghost which is given unto us. (Romans 5:5)

Corrie's love wasn't strong enough to love that prison guard, but God's love was. God filled Corrie's heart with His love for that man, and broke down the barrier between them.

> For he is our peace, who hath made both one, and hath broken down the middle wall of partition between us. (Ephesians 2:14)

CHAPTER 5

BE ENCOURAGED!

David encouraged himself in the LORD his God.
(1 Samuel 30:6)

A FTER fighting the Amalakites, David and his men returned to Ziklag to find their wives and children had been taken captive by their enemies, and their homes were burned. As a result of this tragedy, David's men turned against him:

> And David was greatly distressed; for the people spake of stoning him, because the soul of all the people was grieved, every man for his sons and for his daughters: but David encouraged himself in the LORD his God. (1 Samuel 30:6)

Immediately after this, David's men experienced a radical change. Instead of stoning him, they followed him and overtook their enemies. They rescued their families and returned with animals and other plunder.

How could David, who was cornered and about to be stoned to death, turn around and inspire these angry, grieving, tired men to successfully undertake this? What brought about such a transformation in David and his men?

We can find some keys in the psalms, which record David's prayer and worship. They show us how David encouraged himself in the Lord, and how we can do the same.

In Psalm 42, David talked to his soul (his mind, his will, and his emotions):

> Why art thou cast down, O my soul? and why art thou disquieted in me? hope thou in God: for I shall yet praise him for the help of his countenance. (Psalm 42:5)

The term "cast down" is significant. David was a shepherd. A "cast" sheep is one unable to get back up on its legs. If the shepherd doesn't find the sheep and help it get back on its feet, the sheep will die.

David says his soul is like a cast sheep. He talks to his soul, telling it to get back up on its feet again, to hope in God, and to praise Him.

In Psalm 103, David tells his soul to bless the Lord. Then he reminds himself about God's mercy and love and faithfulness:

> Bless the LORD, O my soul: and all that is within me, bless his holy name. Bless the LORD, O my soul, and forget not all his benefits: Who forgiveth all thine iniquities; who healeth all thy diseases; Who redeemeth thy life from destruction; who crowneth thee with lovingkindness and tender mercies; Who satisfieth thy mouth with good things; so that thy youth is renewed like the eagle's. (Psalm 103:1-5)

At the end of the psalm, he exhorts all of God's creatures to bless Him:

> Bless the LORD, ye his angels, that excel in strength, that do his commandments, hearkening unto the voice of his

word. Bless ye the LORD, all ye his hosts; ye ministers of his, that do his pleasure. Bless the LORD, all his works in all places of his dominion: bless the LORD, O my soul. (Psalm 103:20-22)

In Psalm 104, David tells his soul to bless the Lord:

Bless the LORD, O my soul. O LORD my God, thou art very great; thou art clothed with honour and majesty. (Psalm 104:1)

After that, he praises God for His might and His greatness. In the process, David reminds himself of reasons for blessing the Lord. Look at some of these reasons, and see why David was so compelled to praise the Lord:

Who coverest thyself with light as with a garment: who stretchest out the heavens like a curtain. (vs. 2)

Who maketh his angels spirits; his ministers a flaming fire. (vs. 4)

Who laid the foundations of the earth, that it should not be removed for ever. (vs. 5)

He sendeth the springs into the valleys, which run among the hills. (vs. 10)

He watereth the hills from his chambers: the earth is satisfied with the fruit of thy works. (vs. 13)

He causeth the grass to grow for the cattle, and herb for the service of man. (vs. 14)

The high hills are a refuge for the wild goats; and the rocks for the conies. (vs. 18)

He appointed the moon for seasons: the sun knoweth his going down. (vs. 19)

Thou sendest forth thy spirit, they are created: and thou renewest the face of the earth. (vs. 30)

In Psalm 116, David tells why he loves the Lord, and he exhorts his soul to be at rest. Then he addresses God, giving some reasons for his gratitude:

Return unto thy rest, O my soul; for the LORD hath dealt bountifully with thee. For thou hast delivered my soul from death, mine eyes from tears, and my feet from falling. (Psalm 116:7-8)

Psalm 146 is another example of David exhorting his soul to praise God:

Praise ye the LORD. Praise the LORD, O my soul. While I live will I praise the LORD: I will sing praises unto my God while I have any being. (Psalm 146:1-2)

Bless the Lord at All Times

In Psalm 34, David makes a decision to bless the Lord at all times, no matter what is happening in his life. We can do the same thing:

I will bless the LORD at all times: his praise shall continually be in my mouth. My soul shall make her boast in the LORD: the humble shall hear thereof, and be glad. O magnify the LORD with me, and let us exalt his name together. (Psalm 34:1-3)

Years ago, my husband had a massive heart attack. The phrase "I will bless the LORD at all times" came to my mind while I was in the hospital waiting to see whether or not he would survive. As a result, I spent the time while waiting singing hymns and worship songs instead of worrying. My husband survived, and God gave both of us joy in that hospital in spite of the circumstances.

The apostle Paul also exhorts his listeners to bless the Lord at all times. He encourages them to sing songs of worship and praise and to rejoice in the Lord:

> Speaking to yourselves in psalms and hymns and spiritual songs, singing and making melody in your heart to the Lord; Giving thanks always for all things unto God and the Father in the name of our Lord Jesus Christ. (Ephesians 5:19-20)

> Let the word of Christ dwell in you richly in all wisdom; teaching and admonishing one another in psalms and hymns and spiritual songs, singing with grace in your hearts to the Lord. And whatsoever ye do in word or deed, do all in the name of the Lord Jesus, giving thanks to God and the Father by him. (Colossians 3:16-17)

> Rejoice in the Lord alway: and again I say, Rejoice. (Philippians 4:4)

Paul practiced what he preached. He and Silas were attacked by a mob. Then the Romans gave them a severe beating with rods (with "many stripes") and put them in prison with their feet in the stocks.

Did Paul and Silas complain, saying "God, why did You let this happen to us?" No. They prayed and sang praises to God—loudly enough for the other prisoners to hear them (Acts 16:22-25).

And how did God respond? There was an earthquake, and the prison doors opened, and they were set free from their fetters. This affected the man in charge of the prison so much that he and his household were converted and baptized (Acts 16:26-34).

If you had been whipped like Paul—with your back torn open, bleeding and painful, and then thrown into a filthy prison with your feet in the stocks (which is painful)—would you feel like singing and praising God? I sure wouldn't.

If, like David, you faithfully served a powerful leader (Saul), who instead of appreciating it, tried to murder you and hunted you like an animal, would you feel like blessing the Lord? I wouldn't. That definitely does not come naturally.

Both Paul and David demonstrated it is possible to bless the Lord with thanksgiving. And God doesn't play favorites. He is willing to give us the grace to do the same kinds of things.

Therefore, if we truly desire to "rejoice always" and "give thanks in all circumstances," then God will enable us to do it. And, like Paul and Silas, we may see amazing results when we do.

If we don't really desire to do it, then we can ask God to change our hearts so we want to praise and thank Him no matter what happens to us.

What God has done for us is far more important and far more lasting than anything that people or circumstances can do to us. As a result, it is reasonable (in addition to being biblical) to thank and praise God while we are enduring pain and hardship.

Paul went through great suffering, including being whipped, beaten with rods, stoned, shipwrecked, and imprisoned. Yet he called all of that a "light affliction" because he saw it in terms of eternity rather than our brief time here on Earth. Paul focused on the long-term fruit that God was bringing as a result of his suffering rather than focusing on the pain of the moment.

God's grace is sufficient for us (2 Corinthians 12:9). He is willing and able to give us that same eternal perspective, which results in gratitude, thanksgiving, and praise, in spite of our circumstances.

CHAPTER 6

COMMON SENSE & THE BIBLE

WE can't live biblically unless we have confidence the Bible means what it says, that it is reliable, and that it is credible.

Many problems people have with Scripture are caused by heeding Scripture "experts" who don't use common sense. For example, Jesus gave the "Sermon on the Mount" and the "Sermon on the Plain." Some "experts" consider that to be a contradiction. Was it a mount or a plain?

They have forgotten something. Jesus was a traveling preacher who taught for three years. Therefore, He taught from many mounts and many plains and from ships and seashores and in houses and from every kind of place a person could preach from.

Similarly, some people raise questions because Matthew, Mark, Luke, and John have different versions of a particular parable or teaching. Again, they have forgotten that Jesus was a preacher. And in real life, traveling preachers use the same teachings and illustrations many times, with small variations in how they present them.

Some people are troubled if Matthew, Mark, Luke, or John have differences in how they relate something that happened. For example, with the blind beggar Bartimaeus, one of the

Gospels mentions two blind men, but the others only mention one blind man.

In real life, if you had four people witness an event and write about it, you would have variations in the reports. Different people would focus on different things. So, with the four Gospels, we have four independent eyewitnesses (inspired by the Holy Spirit) writing of their observations rather than four storytellers comparing notes and copying from one another.

As far as the number of blind men goes, there were many beggars on the roadsides, and some of them were blind. It would not be unusual for a blind beggar like Bartimaeus to have friends who were also blind beggars, and in his company. So one account mentions Bartimaeus' fellow beggar, and the other accounts don't. There is nothing unusual about that. It's the kind of thing that usually happens in real life, and therefore adds credence to the four accounts.

Another thing that causes problems for some people is differences of writing style in Paul's letters. In real life, writing style and vocabulary depends on whom we are writing to and on the subject matter. We should expect Paul to write to Gentiles differently than he writes to Jews. We should expect him to write to mature Christians differently than he writes to immature Christians who are having a lot of problems. We should expect him to write to Timothy (a fellow minister who was close to him) differently than he would write to people he hasn't met. The Holy Spirit knew what should be written to different people.

Think about your own letters and e-mails. Would you write to your boss the same way you write to your son or your daughter? Would you write to a nonbeliever the same way that you write to your pastor? Would you write about a football game the same way you write about a research project you are doing at school?

Sometimes Greek verb tenses can cause confusion. For example, 1 John 1:8 says, "If we say that we have no sin, we deceive ourselves, and the truth is not in us." So John is saying that we all sin. But later, in 1 John 3:6, he says, "Whosoever abideth in him sinneth not: whosoever sinneth hath not seen him, neither known him." Now that could be confusing. The problem is the Greek verb tense. First John 3:6 is saying that if we abide in Him, we do not keep on sinning—it's not a one-time event but a lifestyle. Any Christian can sin and repent. That is very different from purposefully making a habit of sinning or living continually in sin.

Some scholars say the Sermon on the Mount is a compilation of teachings rather than one sermon. They have forgotten something. We live in a televised world where many people have short attention spans, and many preachers have short sermons. Back in 1858, when Abraham Lincoln debated Stephen Douglas (the famous Lincoln-Douglas Debates), each debate lasted for three hours. So people in those days were able to do serious listening for three hours straight.

I did an experiment. I read the entire Sermon on the Mount out loud at a slow, conversational pace. (It's the Gospel of Matthew, chapters 5 through 7.) It only took 15 minutes. Surely Jesus preached longer than that to people who may have traveled several-days' journey to listen to him. He was only going to be with those particular people one time. So He had to get as much truth to them as He could during that one time of preaching.

We know that Jesus and His followers did some lengthy preaching. On one occasion, the apostle Paul preached all night long, until daybreak (Acts 20:7-12).

Therefore, I would expect that what the Bible gives us from the Sermon on the Mount is only a selection out of many teachings Jesus gave on that occasion. And the quotations from Jesus that we have may only be the conclusions He gave following longer teachings about those issues:

> And there are also many other things which Jesus did, the which, if they should be written every one, I suppose that even the world itself could not contain the books that should be written. (John 21:25)

Matthew's account of the Sermon on the Mount is the result of the Holy Spirit showing Matthew which of the many teachings Jesus gave should be included in the report and which statements Jesus made should be quoted. It is also the result of the Holy Spirit enabling Matthew to remember accurately. Jesus promised His disciples:

> But the Comforter, which is the Holy Ghost, whom the Father will send in my name, he shall teach you all things, and bring all things to your remembrance, whatsoever I have said unto you. (John 14:26)

Jesus' Teachings Made Sense

Matthew 5:38-42 is a good opportunity to use some common sense. Jesus basically told people to be loving and forgiving instead of quarreling and vengeful. For example, He said:

> Ye have heard that it hath been said, An eye for an eye, and a tooth for a tooth: But I say unto you, That ye resist not evil: but whosoever shall smite thee on thy right cheek, turn to him the other also. (Matthew 5:38-39)

First he said, don't try to get revenge. Then he said to allow someone to slap you on the cheek. Being slapped is unpleasant, but it is a relatively mild degree of pain and hardship. Jesus did not say that Christians should passively allow people to rape their wives and murder their children. He didn't even tell Christians to passively submit to persecution. He said:

> But when they persecute you in this city, flee ye into another. (Matthew 10:23)

Jesus also said that if someone sues us for our tunic, we should let them have it, and even our cloak as well (Matthew 5:40). That is just some clothing. Although clothing was more difficult to obtain back in those days than it is now, it was still just clothing. Jesus did not say we should allow people to take our home and our farm or business so we and our family become homeless and destitute. By comparing Scripture with Scripture, we can see that Jesus had a very balanced view of how to live at peace with our fellow man.

Here is another example of interpreting Scripture with Scripture. It also comes from the Sermon on the Mount. Jesus said:

> Judge not, that ye be not judged. (Matthew 7:1)

Some people interpret this as meaning we should never criticize anything that other people say or do. However, that cannot be the meaning of this passage because later on in the same chapter Jesus said:

> Beware of false prophets, which come to you in sheep's clothing, but inwardly they are ravening wolves. Ye shall know them by their fruits. Do men gather grapes of thorns, or figs of thistles? Even so every good tree bringeth forth good fruit; but a corrupt tree bringeth forth evil fruit. (Matthew 7:15-17)

How can we beware of them if we can't recognize them? How can we warn our friends and family to beware of them if we aren't allowed to say anything negative about anybody? According to what Jesus said, He expects us to be able to recognize false teachers and to discern the difference between good and bad fruit in a person's life.

How do we reconcile that with not judging people? According to my study Bible, Jesus warned us against condemning the motives of others because only God knows their hearts and their motives. We cannot condemn people. However, we are expected to be "fruit inspectors" who can tell the difference between people who teach Christian truth and people who teach a false gospel (Matthew

7:15-20). This is why Paul did not hesitate to name names when it came to identifying those who teach destructive heresy (2 Timothy 2:17). In addition, Jesus commanded us to "judge righteous judgment" (John 7:24).

Here is a practical example from real life. If we have reasons to question someone's morality and their level of responsible behavior, we cannot condemn them because only God knows their heart. However, we should not let them babysit our children. And it would be foolish to become business partners with them.

In conclusion, if we come across a passage in Scripture that doesn't make sense to us, we can ask God to help us understand it. If we pray and give that passage further consideration, and we still can't understand it, then we can just set it aside and go on reading. There have been times when a Scripture passage I didn't understand before suddenly made sense. It's like a light goes on, and I can see it.

Reading Scripture is a lifetime adventure. What we do understand is more than enough to guide us and help us know the Lord and His ways better. Let's use what we can understand and trust God to take care of the rest of it in His own good timing.

CHAPTER 7

THE TRAIN STATION

Enter ye in at the strait [narrow] gate: for wide is the gate, and broad is the way, that leadeth to destruction, and many there be which go in thereat: Because strait is the gate, and narrow is the way, which leadeth unto life, and few there be that find it. (Matthew 7:13-14)

LIFE on planet Earth is similar to being in a train station. No matter what happens here, the most important thing is to take the right train to the right destination.

Will we take the Glory Train to Heaven? Or will we take the other train, which goes to Hell?

Back in the 1960s, I would often take a train from Washington, D.C. in order to visit my mom's parents in New York City and my dad's parents in Connecticut. The train stations were busy, noisy places with a lot going on.

I would go to the station, get a seat, and listen for the loud speaker to announce "Train now leaving for New York on track ___." Those announcements were often difficult to hear because of the noise and because the quality of the sound was not good. In addition, some of the announcers spoke rapidly and were difficult to understand. As a result, I really had to focus on listening carefully in order to catch my train. If I was not at the right track at the right time, then I would miss it.

While waiting in train stations, sometimes I would be sitting next to pleasant people who wanted to talk. At other times, the people around me had no interest in fellow passengers. Occasionally, I would be within hearing distance of unpleasant people who talked about immoral things, using nasty language. When that happened, I was a captive audience unless I could find a seat somewhere else.

One time, I was in a small station in Virginia that was so busy I wound up having to stand the entire time. That was no fun. It was tiring and hard on my feet even though I was young at the time. It would have been a real hardship for an older person who had health problems.

Some people had children with them, including babies. They had to keep track of their children, comfort restless babies, and still carefully listen for the announcement of their train.

Modern train stations have big screens showing what track a train is on. As a result, travelers don't have to depend on hearing what is said during a brief announcement. Instead, one can look at the screens at any time to find out what is going on. But back then, it was very different. Everything depended on hearing that announcement.

No matter what was going on in the station in general and with me personally, the most important thing was to get to the right track at the right time in order to get on the right train for the right destination. Everything else was very secondary.

Did it matter whether I had a pleasant time or a difficult time while waiting for the train? Of course it did. It was right to do whatever I could to get a good seat, be around nice people, and have something to eat if I became hungry. But the important thing was to get on the right train and arrive at the right destination. Compared to that, everything else was of little importance. I might have a nice time while waiting, or I might have to endure some physical or emotional hardship. But whatever the case, the essential thing was to get on the right train.

As I said before, planet Earth is like a train station. There are two trains with two very different destinations. One is the Glory Train that goes to Heaven; the other is the train to Hell that a country song calls the "long black train."[3]

Like a train station, life on Earth is busy, with a lot of different things going on at the same time. It is easy to become so engrossed in those things we forget that one of these days we will leave Earth and go to Heaven or Hell. It is easy to get so caught up in the day-to-day busyness that we forget about eternity.

There is a simple key to dealing with the things that cause us to become frustrated, discouraged, or fearful: We need to keep the big picture in mind.

We need to make a conscious effort to see things in terms of eternity. That will give us the right perspective. And having that perspective will impact what we do, how we feel, and how we respond to hardship and trials of various kinds.

CHAPTER 8

FOUR KINDS OF SOIL

But that on the good ground are they, which in an honest and good heart, having heard the word, keep it, and bring forth fruit with patience. (Luke 8:15)

F OR me, one of the most discouraging problems is seeing people I love dearly do self-destructive things; I love them, but I can't help them. And that is just heartbreaking.

Two years ago, this happened with an old friend named Tom.* We have been friends for over twenty years. When I met him, he had gotten out of the occult and out of taking drugs (primarily marijuana), and he had his own landscaping business. That was quite an achievement. We attended the same church, and he became close friends with my family, especially with my mom and dad, because he came from a very dysfunctional family and needed a mom and dad in his life. Tom also did our yard work and took care of our plants, so we saw him regularly. He would often come into the house to chat after doing his work.

---

* Not his real name.

Tom loved God, and we often talked about things of the Lord or things we all had been seeing in Scripture. In addition, we talked about personal matters, and Tom told us about many difficult things that had happened in his life. We were like an adopted family to share his love for the Lord, to be understanding about his problems, and to encourage him in any way we could. And, of course, we all always gave him lots of warm hugs. We also prayed together.

When my mother and father both died, that was hard on Tom. Then as the economy went downhill, his business wasn't doing as well. (When people are pinched for funds, one thing they can afford to do without is landscaping.) Then he had some personal problems. And then somebody killed one of his cats with a knife and left its body where Tom would be sure to see it. After that happened, I noticed that when Tom came by to talk, he wasn't making good sense any more. He was saying weird things, and his thinking seemed to be strange. I finally asked him if he was smoking pot again, and he was. Of course, that affected the quality of his landscaping, and as a result his business suffered even more to the point he eventually had to go out of business and leave the area to live with a relative.

Many people don't seem to understand how deadly smoking pot can be. It really affects both the mind and the judgment. Back in my college days, I tried to help a young man named Eddie who took drugs. One time he and I were crossing a busy four-lane street at night, and Eddie was stoned on pot. He stopped in the middle of the street to look at the headlights of the oncoming cars and said, "Wow!" He just loved the way those lights looked, and he stood there watching them. It never occurred to him they were attached to cars that could run him over. If I hadn't been there to physically pull Eddie over to the sidewalk, he probably would have been hit by a car.

In addition, taking any kind of mind-altering drugs can open people up to demonic influence. There is a reason why witch doctors, sorcerers, witches, and satanists take drugs. They want to tap into that dark spiritual connection because they think it will give them power and enable them to do things. Well it does, but they will pay a terrible hellish price for it.

I lost a lot of sleep over Tom and did a lot of crying because of his backsliding. I prayed for him and gave him some biblically based advice. Last year, I saw some real improvement, but I think he has gone downhill again. He stopped contacting me, and I think it's because he's smoking pot again and he doesn't want me to know it.

This year, a woman who was a close friend for over twelve years became self-destructive in various ways and abruptly ended our friendship, totally cutting herself off from me. That has also been so heartbreaking for me. The grief and distress actually aggravated some health problems I had. This woman knows the Bible well, and we used to have wonderful conversations about the Lord, as well as praying together. She has the head knowledge, but she isn't living by what she knows. Her behavior is what the Bible calls living by the flesh, as opposed to living by the Spirit. The Bible says:

> For if ye *live after the flesh, ye shall die:* but if ye through the Spirit do mortify the deeds of the body, ye shall live. For as many as are led by the Spirit of God, they are the sons of God. (Romans 8:13-14, emphasis added)

> The night is far spent, the day is at hand: let us therefore cast off the works of darkness, and let us put on the armour of light. Let us walk honestly, as in the day; not in rioting and drunkenness, not in chambering [sexual immorality] and wantonness, not in strife and envying. But put ye on the Lord Jesus Christ, and *make not provision for the flesh, to fulfil the lusts thereof.* (Romans 13:12-14, emphasis added)

Notice some of the things that living by the flesh results in are obviously wrong, such as drunkenness and sexual immorality. But also notice that "strife" and "envy" are listed right along with those more obvious sins.

Galatians speaks of a war between our flesh and the Spirit. Then it lists the fruit of the flesh and the fruit of the Spirit. Although these are part of one long passage, I'm breaking it into four sections: the war, the "fruit" of the flesh, the fruit of the Spirit, and an exhortation.

This Scripture passage mentions "lust" several times. In our modern world, the word "lust" is usually used about sexual things. However, it really means strong desires. People can have a lust for many kinds of things including fame, power, money, or wanting people's approval at any price. Paul says:

> For the flesh lusteth against the Spirit, and the Spirit against the flesh: and these are contrary the one to the other: so that ye cannot do the things that ye would. (Galatians 5:17)

> Now the works of the flesh are manifest, which are these; Adultery, fornication, uncleanness, lasciviousness, Idolatry, witchcraft, hatred, variance [discord, contentiousness], emulations [jealousy], wrath, strife, seditions [dissensions], heresies, Envyings, murders, drunkenness, revellings, and such like: of the which I tell you before, as I have also told you in time past, that they which do such things shall not inherit the kingdom of God. (Galatians 5:19-21)

> But the fruit of the Spirit is love, joy, peace, long-suffering, gentleness, goodness, faith, Meekness, temperance: against such there is no law. (Galatians 5:22-23)

> And they that are Christ's have crucified the flesh with the affections and lusts. If we live in the Spirit, let us also walk in the Spirit. (Galatians 5:24-25)

In the case of the old friend who terminated our friendship, I believe the problem is long-term anger and bitterness. Some terrible things were done to her many years ago, and she has never really been able to forgive the people who did it. That long-term anger has caused her a lot of damage. The Bible warns us:

> Be ye angry, and sin not: let not the sun go down upon your wrath: Neither give place to the devil. (Ephesians 4:26-27)

The term "place" here is a military term that means a beachhead. It's a place from which an enemy can launch an assault. Therefore, long-term anger enables the devil to influence us, to tempt us, and to torment us. It also enables him to put pressure on us to do things that will harm the people closest to us. In this case, my old friend is harming herself and her daughter, and she has broken my heart. I have been so frustrated and discouraged because I cannot help her. I want to warn her about the dangers of long-term anger and unforgiveness, but she has cut off all communication with me, so I'm not able to do that.

Finally, I realized something. A year ealier I had given her my book *How to Prepare for Hard Times and Persecution*, which includes a long chapter titled "Don't Give the Devil a Beachhead" that warns about the dangers of long-term anger and unforgiveness. So I did tell her, but it was in writing rather than in person. She knows better, but she isn't living according to what she knows.

Why? The answer to that question lies in the parable of the sower and the four kinds of soil. And I can't begin to tell you what a relief it was for me when I realized that.

I know that many other Christians have been through similar kinds of heartache. That's why I'm writing about it.

Jesus gave the parable of the sower and the four kinds of soil. Then His disciples asked Him what it meant, and He explained it to them, saying:

> A sower went out to sow his seed: and as he sowed, some fell by the way side; and it was trodden down, and the fowls of the air devoured it. And some fell upon a rock;

and as soon as it was sprung up, it withered away, because it lacked moisture. And some fell among thorns; and the thorns sprang up with it, and choked it. And other fell on good ground, and sprang up, and bare fruit an hundredfold. And when he had said these things, he cried, He that hath ears to hear, let him hear. (Luke 8:5-8)

Now the parable is this: The seed is the word of God. Those by the way side are they that hear; then cometh the devil, and taketh away the word out of their hearts, lest they should believe and be saved. They on the rock are they, which, when they hear, receive the word with joy; and these have no root, which for a while believe, and in time of temptation fall away. And that which fell among thorns are they, which, when they have heard, go forth, and are choked with cares and riches and pleasures of this life, and bring no fruit to perfection. But that on the good ground are they, which in an honest and good heart, having heard the word, keep it, and bring forth fruit with patience. (Luke 8:11-15)

Notice the sower did the right thing, and the seed was good seed. The reason for the difference in results was the nature of the soil the seed was planted in.

The second kind of soil is described as "rock." That cannot be solid rock, because in that case, the plant would not have been able to grow at all. Rather, it must be a relatively thin layer of soil that has rock underneath it. Therefore, the roots of the plant can't go down deep enough to keep the plant alive during a time of testing.

Notice that with this second kind of soil, initially the people "receive the word with joy." And then when the trials come, they wither and die.

Have you ever seen this happen? I have, and it's tragic. I know people who seemed to love God and love the Bible. They were so enthusiastic about the things of God. And then years later, after they have been through some rough times, they are no longer living biblically. They are just going through the motions at church, but it's habit rather than being life-changing conviction. And you wonder, "How did they get from there to where I see them now?" Well, the answer is the ground looked good, but there were rocks underneath the topsoil that was on the surface.

What are those rocks? Long-term anger and unforgiveness are big ones. They are hard and unyielding. And there can be other things we refuse to allow God to deal with. If we don't let Him deal with them, then we are refusing to allow Him to be Lord of every area of our lives. That is a form of rebellion, and it is sinful. Therefore, we need to develop the habit of asking God to search our hearts and change whatever needs to be changed. David said:

> Who can understand his errors? cleanse thou me from secret faults. Keep back thy servant also from presumptuous sins; let them not have dominion over me: then shall I be upright, and I shall be innocent from the great transgression. Let the words of my mouth, and the meditation of my heart, be acceptable in thy sight, O Lord, my strength, and my redeemer. (Psalm 19:12-14)

What about the third kind of soil? Notice that the thorns are "cares and riches and pleasures of this life." That includes being overly concerned about money. The Bible warns us:

> For the love of money is the root of all evil: which while some coveted after, they have erred from the faith, and pierced themselves through with many sorrows. (1 Timothy 6:10)

Notice that it isn't the money itself that's the problem. It's the love of money—wanting it too badly and being too focused on it.

"Cares" includes worrying about people we know, about the state of this world, and about our own future. I have to fight that all the time because I'm acutely aware of what is going on in the world today. That can really weigh me down. As a result, I need to spend more time in prayer and worship in order to balance it.

"Pleasures of this life" includes entertainment. How many Christians spend hours every day watching TV or chatting on Facebook, but they can't find fifteen minutes to read the Bible? We have become a society that is addicted to entertainment. Have you noticed how often in restaurants you see people sitting at the same table, but instead of talking with one another, they are texting or checking their e-mails?

Christians are not immune to this. It might take a different form. For example, I hope Christians watch decent shows instead of those featuring sex and violence. But even with decent shows, it can still be a diversion that makes us less fruitful. And carried too far, it can prevent us from bearing any fruit at all.

We see this in personal relationships. It used to be that meal time was when the family talked together and shared their hearts with one another. Relationships have to be nurtured. If you don't do that, they dry up. In these days, how many families watch TV while they are eating instead of talking to one another? That could have a lot to do with why so many children are rebellious and why so many marriages end in divorce.

Many things are fine in moderation. For example, good quality ice cream and home-made cookies. I love both of them. But if you overdo them, you can ruin your health. Not only will you gain weight, but you can wind up becoming diabetic or having other health problems. The same principle applies to entertainment. In moderation, it is fine. But if we overdo it, it harms us.

Then there is the fourth kind of soil. Notice it requires an "honest" heart. That means someone who loves the truth. In other words, he wants the truth at any price. He would rather deal with difficult and unpleasant truth than go into denial or wishful thinking. We need to have a love for the truth.

We also need to have patience. *Webster's Dictionary* defines "patience" as "the capacity, habit, or fact of being patient." So this is habitual, a way of life. The dictionary defines "patient" as the following:

1. Bearing pains or trials calmly or without complaint
2. Manifesting forbearance under provocation or strain
3. Not hasty or impetuous
4. Steadfast despite opposition, difficulty, or adversity

These are character traits every Christian needs to develop. That means making a decision to develop them and working on it diligently, and most importantly, asking God to help us do it.

Notice that patience is the very first quality Paul lists when describing what real love is. In the following Scripture passage, "charity" means "love." It is described as being long suffering, which is another way of saying "patient." Also notice the last verse says that love bears all things and endures all things. That is another description of patience. So Paul's description of love begins and ends with patience. He says:

> Charity suffereth long, and is kind; charity envieth not; charity vaunteth not itself, is not puffed up, Doth not behave itself unseemly, seeketh not her own, is not easily provoked, thinketh no evil; Rejoiceth not in iniquity, but rejoiceth in the truth; Beareth all things, believeth all things, hopeth all things, endureth all things. (1 Corinthians 13:4-7)

How important is love? According to Jesus, it should be the defining characteristic of a Christian. He said:

> By this shall all men know that ye are my disciples, if ye have love one to another. (John 13:35)

The apostle John said that if anybody claims to love God but doesn't love his brothers and sisters in Christ, then he is a liar. That doesn't necessarily mean he is consciously telling a lie. There could be self-deception involved. He might be a pastor or a worship leader who is harsh and unloving with his own family, doing hurtful things to them. I know a worship leader who turned out that way, and it was devastating, especially for his children. John said:

> If a man say, I love God, and hateth his brother, he is a liar: for he that loveth not his brother whom he hath seen, how can he love God whom he hath not seen? (1 John 4:20)

Now most Christians would never carry it to the extent that worship leader did, but all of us need to be on guard. It is too easy to take people for granted and fail to treat them well, as described in 1 Corinthians 13.

We can ask God to put His love in our hearts, to give us His love for people. Paul said:

> And hope maketh not ashamed; because the love of God is shed abroad in our hearts by the Holy Ghost which is given unto us. (Romans 5:5)

We need to keep on praying for that because we need to keep growing in love. It's a process; it takes time. The important thing is, what direction are we moving in? Are we becoming more and more loving? In our own strength, we cannot become all that God desires us to become, but He promises to give us what we need to live godly lives.

> Grace and peace be multiplied unto you through the knowledge of God, and of Jesus our Lord, according as his divine power hath given unto us all things that pertain unto life and godliness. (2 Peter 1:2-3)

CHAPTER 9

CASTING OUR CARES ON GOD

Humble yourselves therefore under the mighty hand of God, that he may exalt you in due time: Casting all your care upon him; for he careth for you." (1 Peter 5:6-7)

In the last chapter, we noted how the parable of the sower reveals a condition (the third kind of soil) that can be especially problematic for the Christian who is trying to serve the Lord and be fruitful for the Kingdom—namely that of seed sown among thorns (weeds) that would choke out one's effectiveness. In explaining this part of the parable, Jesus said:

> And these are they which are sown among thorns; such as hear the word, And *the cares of this world,* and the deceitfulness of riches, and the lusts of other things entering in, choke the word, and it becometh unfruitful. (Mark 4:18-19, emphasis added)

It is obvious that things like lust for money and power, and sexual immorality would prevent Christians from bearing fruit for the Kingdom of God. But Jesus also included "the cares of this world" in the list of "weeds" that are deadly enough to prevent the plant from bearing fruit. Therefore, we cannot afford to be overcome by "cares" (fear, anxiety, worry, etc.). Jesus expects us to bear fruit for His Kingdom. And we want to be fruitful for Him.

Peter implies that if we fail to cast our cares on God, then we open ourselves up to spiritual warfare. I'll repeat the opening Scripture of this chapter, and add the two verses that come immediately after it. Peter says:

> Humble yourselves therefore under the mighty hand of God, that he may exalt you in due time: Casting all your care upon him; for he careth for you. Be sober, be vigilant; because your adversary the devil, as a roaring lion, walketh about, seeking whom he may devour: Whom resist stedfast in the faith, knowing that the same afflictions are accomplished in your brethren that are in the world. (1 Peter 5:6-9)

What happens when we become anxious, worried, and full of cares? Our emotions take over. We act impulsively. We lose sleep, and lose our tempers, and so on. We get so focused on our worries we fail to notice, or take care of, important things in our lives. Well, that is the exact opposite of being "sober" and "alert." And therefore, we are not in good shape to resist the attacks of the devil.

James said something that relates to part of what Peter said in the quote above:

> But he giveth more grace. Wherefore he saith, God resisteth the proud, but giveth grace unto the humble. Submit yourselves therefore to God. Resist the devil, and he will flee from you. (James 4:6-7)

How do we submit to God? One important way is by taking His Word seriously and trying to live the way the Bible tells us to live. And that includes not being anxious. Paul said:

> Be careful for nothing; but in every thing by prayer and supplication with thanksgiving let your requests be made known unto God. (Philippians 4:6)

In the *King James*, the word "careful" means "full of care." In other words, "anxious." So Paul's point is that we should be praying instead of worrying. We need to give our cares to God. That includes fears for ourselves and for those we love. For example, parents whose children are soldiers fighting overseas have valid reasons to fear for the safety of their children.

We all become afraid at times. The problem occurs when we allow that fear to take over. Going back to the parable of the sower and the four kinds of soil, when weeds first begin to grow, if you pull them up by the roots, they won't cause any significant harm to the plant. However, if you let them keep growing, then the weeds can choke the plant and prevent it from bearing fruit. In some cases, weeds can even kill the plant. I had some beautiful azaleas that were killed by ivy.

> Worry does not deprive tomorrow of its sorrow. It deprives today of its strength.
> (Corrie ten Boom)

The principle is similar to avoiding long-term anger. God understands that at times, we will become angry, but the point is we cannot afford to remain angry. Otherwise, we may give the devil a beachhead ("place") in which to attack us as we discussed in chapter 8.

Similarly, we can't help getting anxious at times. However, we cannot afford to remain anxious. We need to remind ourselves that God is faithful, and He loves us, and He will take good care of us. His grace is sufficient for us. And He will make *everything* work out for our long-term, eternal good if we love Him. No exceptions (Romans 8:28).

Praise and worship are a good way to remind ourselves that God is good, that He loves us, and that we can trust Him. David said:

> O magnify the Lord with me, and let us exalt his name together. (Psalm 34:3)

The term "magnify" can't mean making God any bigger than He already is, because that is impossible since God is already infinite. Therefore, it must mean making ourselves become more aware of how great God really is. In other words, as we focus on God and on His greatness, His goodness, His mercy, and His lovingkindness, then He appears greater in our eyes. And because of that, our problems seem so much smaller.

So what we are really doing is seeing things in proper proportion. In reality, any problem we could face is so small compared to God and His great love for us. For God, even death is small by comparison (1 Corinthians 15:53-55). He raised Jesus from the dead; and some day He will raise all believers from the dead.

We need to get our focus off our problems and on to God. On a practical note, we need to be aware of the problems and do whatever we can in practical terms to deal with them. However, when it comes to our emotions and our thoughts, our primary focus needs to be on the Lord God Almighty. The apostle Paul told us:

> Finally, brethren, whatsoever things are true, whatsoever things are honest, whatsoever things are just, whatsoever things are pure, whatsoever things are lovely, whatsoever things are of good report; if there be any virtue, and if there be any praise, think on these things. (Philippians 4:8)

True, honest, just, pure, lovely (beautiful), good, virtuous, and worthy of praise are all attributes of God. So although we need to be aware of the bad stuff in our lives and do whatever we can to deal with it, our primary focus should be on God Himself. The Bible says it is the life of Christ in us that gives us the power and strength we need. When we are born again, He lives in us (abides in us), and it is His life that changes and transforms us.

> I am crucified with Christ: nevertheless I live; yet not I, but Christ liveth in me. (Galatians 2:20)

> . . . to whom God would make known what is the riches of the glory of this mystery among the Gentiles; *which is Christ in you*, the hope of glory. (Colossians 1:27, emphasis added)

When you drive your car, you look at the road ahead of you. You quickly check the mirrors, and you see sideways with your peripheral vision, but your primary focus has to be on the road that is directly ahead of you. Likewise, we can focus on God and look at the bad stuff with our peripheral vision. That will make it easier to cast our cares (concerns about the bad stuff) on God and leave them in His hands, trusting that He will take care of things in the right way—and in the right timing.

Casting our cares on God is a skill we can learn and a habit we can develop. We can ask God to teach us how to do it. We can ask Him to make us willing and able to do it. And we can ask Him to teach us not to grab those cares and take them back again after we have given them to Him.

God told us to do it. He wants us to do it. And His grace is sufficient for us. Therefore, He is willing and able to teach us how to do it. God can enable us to make casting our cares on Him become a way of life for us.

It's a process. It can take time. When we succeed in casting a care on Him, then we should thank Him for it. When we fail, then we should repent and ask Him to help us do it.

Human parents teach their children how to do what they expect of them. Would our Heavenly Father do any less for us? Of course not.

The more we cast our cares on God, the more we will learn to trust Him at a deeper level. In addition, we will experience a new degree of peace and joy. That will be a blessing for us and for those who are close to us.

I can do all things through Christ which strengtheneth me. (Philippians 4:13)

BLESSED ASSURANCE
by Fanny Crosby
1873

Blessed assurance, Jesus is mine!
O what a foretaste of glory divine!
Heir of salvation, purchase of God,
Born of His Spirit, washed in His blood.

This is my story, this is my song,
Praising my Savior all the day long;
This is my story, this is my song,
Praising my Savior all the day long.

Perfect submission, perfect delight,
Visions of rapture now burst on my sight;
Angels descending bring from above,
Echoes of mercy, whispers of love.

This is my story, this is my song,
Praising my Savior all the day long;
This is my story, this is my song,
Praising my Savior all the day long.

Perfect submission, all is at rest;
I in my Savior am happy and blest,
Watching and waiting, looking above,
Filled with His goodness, lost in His love...

RADIANT VICTORY!
BY GEORGI P. VINS*

Don't rush tomorrow;
for the day will come
Before you know. . .
It is ordained by Heaven!
Of bread,
I have my daily needed portion,
On rainy days,
I've shelter for my head.

So though my flesh decline
And daily weakens,
From exiles,
Long my heart's
Strong rhythm grows faint,
But still the spirit burns with sacred fire
Without a shade of wav'ring
Or complaint!
But best of all—the light of Jesus' love,
That pierces every age and generation,
On mighty wings of trust
And steady patience
Bears up my soul to radiant victory!

---

* Georgi Vins was a Baptist pastor, imprisoned for his faith in the Soviet Union starting at the age of 32, for a total of eight years for his faith in Christ. This poem was written in 1978 in the Yakutia, Tabaga Prison Camp.

CHAPTER 10

BLESSINGS IN DISGUISE

THE apostle Paul wrote the Colossians a pastoral letter giving them some practical instructions in how to develop godly character. These are guidelines which apply to all Christians, including us. They are based on our relationship with Jesus Christ (Colossians 3:1).

An important aspect of this is setting our minds "on things above, not on things on the earth" (Colossians 3:2). We need to see things from the perspective of Heaven and eternity—as opposed to being primarily focused on what things look and feel like right now, down here on Earth.

Paul tells us to "put to death" and "put off" various kinds of carnal behavior that are sinful and destructive. Among these are sexual immorality, covetousness, anger, and lying (Colossians 3:5-10). Then he tells us how Christians should live. He says:

> Put on therefore, as the elect of God, holy and beloved, bowels of mercies, kindness, humbleness of mind, meekness, longsuffering; Forbearing one another, and forgiving one another, if any man have a quarrel against

any: even as Christ forgave you, so also do ye. And above all these things put on charity [love], which is the bond of perfectness. And let the peace of God rule in your hearts, to the which also ye are called in one body; and be ye thankful. (Colossians 3:12-15)

Paul sums it up by saying:

And whatsoever ye do in word or deed, do all in the name of the Lord Jesus, giving thanks to God and the Father by him. (Colossians 3:17)

If we can't add "in the name of Jesus" to what we say—without dishonoring the Lord by doing it—then we shouldn't say it. Likewise, if we want to do something that Jesus would not want to have His name associated with, then we shouldn't do it.

How can we become people who live like that? How can we act that way consistently enough for it to become a normal, habitual part of our life?

When people want to build up physical strength, they need to work against resistance. That's why people lift weights and do isometric exercises. The process can be uncomfortable at times. That's why there is the saying, "No pain, no gain."

The same principle applies to building godly character. In order to develop patience, we need to be put into situations where patience is required. That gives us the opportunity to develop our "patience muscles." In order to become more forgiving, we need to have things to forgive. That enables us to strengthen our "forgiveness muscles."

In order to become more loving, we need to have people in our lives who are difficult to love. Sometimes that can be quite challenging. When it is, we can ask God to change our hearts and give us His love for these people.

Charles Spurgeon wrote about the importance of loving our neighbors. When discussing the problem of loving difficult people, he said:

> So much the more room for the heroism of love. Wouldst thou be a feather-bed warrior, instead of bearing the rough fight of love? He who dares the most, shall win the most; and if rough be thy path of love, tread it boldly, still loving thy neighbours through thick and thin.[4]

Such trials enable us (by God's grace) to develop character qualities which will bear good fruit for eternity. If we can get a vision for the valuable end results, then we will be able to see the trials as being helpful. That will enable us to "count it all joy"—to consider it something to be grateful for rather than a problem to endure. The apostle James said:

> Wherefore seeing we also are compassed about with so great a cloud of witnesses, let us lay aside every weight, and the sin which doth so easily beset us, and let us run with patience the race that is set before us, Looking unto Jesus the author and finisher of our faith; who for the joy that was set before him endured the cross, despising the shame, and is set down at the right hand of the throne of God. (Hebrews 12:1-2)

Our trials here on Earth are so brief compared with eternity. We can ask God to give us that eternal perspective, so we see them as He does. Then we will be able to understand and appropriate the following statements of the apostles Peter and Paul:

> Beloved, think it not strange concerning the fiery trial which is to try you, as though some strange thing happened unto you: But rejoice, inasmuch as ye are partakers of Christ's

sufferings; that, when his glory shall be revealed, ye may be glad also with exceeding joy. (1 Peter 4:12-13)

For which cause we faint not; but though our outward man perish, yet the inward man is renewed day by day. For our light affliction, which is but for a moment, worketh for us a far more exceeding and eternal weight of glory; While we look not at the things which are seen, but at the things which are not seen: for the things which are seen are temporal; but the things which are not seen are eternal. (2 Corinthians 4:16-18)

In some of the Beatitudes, Jesus called some things "blessings" that don't feel at all like blessings when they happen to us. He said:

Blessed are they that mourn: for they shall be comforted. (Matthew 5:4)

As a widow, I know something about mourning. After my husband died, God comforted and encouraged me through Scripture and during times of prayer. And I have been able to pass that comfort and encouragement on to other people. The apostle Paul wrote about something similar, saying:

Blessed be God, even the Father of our Lord Jesus Christ, the Father of mercies, and the God of all comfort; Who comforteth us in all our tribulation, that we may be able to comfort them which are in any trouble, by the comfort wherewith we ourselves are comforted of God. For as the sufferings of Christ abound in us, so our consolation also aboundeth by Christ. (2 Corinthians 1:3-5)

Here is another Beatitude that doesn't feel like a blessing when we face difficult circumstances. Jesus told us:

Blessed are they which do hunger and thirst after righteousness: for they shall be filled. (Matthew 5:6)

What does it take for somebody to "hunger and thirst after righteousness"? Going through the trial of enduring unrighteous behavior. This can range from relatively mild things to serious crimes. It can involve traumatic one-time events or a series of events. It can be something done to an individual or to a group of people.

How could such a thing turn out to be a blessing? I have heard testimonies of men and women who were so appalled by unrighteous behavior that they longed for truth, justice, goodness, and righteousness. And they found it—in God. They became Christians. God not only satisfied their longing, He also changed their hearts and made them His children.

Here is another difficult Beatitude. This is hard to endure, but it can result in eternal rewards. Jesus said:

Blessed are ye, when men shall hate you, and when they shall separate you from their company, and shall reproach you, and cast out your name as evil, for the Son of man's sake. Rejoice ye in that day, and leap for joy: for, behold, your reward is great in heaven: for in the like manner did their fathers unto the prophets. (Luke 6:22-23)

Could this be a blessing? Yes. Have you ever met Christians from countries with severe persecution? They have a kind of wholehearted love for God that is rare in nations where it is safe to be a Christian. And their zeal for others to know God is so strong that they risk their lives in order to share the Gospel. Their life here on Earth is difficult, but they will have great joy in Heaven for all eternity.

God really does bring good out of everything that happens to people who love Him.

GOD'S LOVE

God, who made the earth,
has always loved us.
Before we drew a breath,
our heart was known.
He created us to live with Him forever,
To sing with joy
and bow before His throne.

Our time on earth is hard,
but it is fleeting.
No matter how things seem,
God's always there.

He'll guide us and protect us
and watch over us,
And take away each fear
and tear and care.

When all the toil
and pain and fear have ended,
When sorrow's gone,
and all we know is love,
Then we and God
will celebrate forever,
Rejoicing with the saints
in Heaven above.

CHAPTER 11

THE IMPORTANCE OF LOVE

And because iniquity shall abound, the love of many shall wax cold. (Matthew 24:12)

ACCORDING to Jesus, the defining mark of being a Christian is love. It isn't going to church, or having great faith, or giving generously to ministries, or doing good works. It is love. Jesus made this very clear when He said:

By this shall all men know that ye are my disciples, if ye have love one to another. (John 13:35)

In addition, the apostle Paul listed a number of things Christians do and said that, without love, those things were of no benefit to them. Paul said that even having tremendous faith, giving everything we have to help the poor, and being killed because we are Christians won't do us any good if we don't have love. (1 Corinthians 13:2-3)

Here is how Paul describes love. Where the *King James Bible* renders it as "charity," Paul means love. These days, the word "charity" is used primarily in terms of things like giving to charities but back when the *King James Bible* was written, it meant love. Charitable giving is only one small aspect of love. Here is how Paul describes love:

> Charity suffereth long, and is kind; charity envieth not; charity vaunteth not itself, is not puffed up, Doth not behave itself unseemly, seeketh not her own, is not easily provoked, thinketh no evil; Rejoiceth not in iniquity, but rejoiceth in the truth; Beareth all things, believeth all things, hopeth all things, endureth all things. (1 Corinthians 13:4-7)

One form that lack of love can take is passivity because love is active. Years of watching television has conditioned many modern Christians into becoming passive spectators instead of active participants. This is the polar opposite of the Bible's description of Christian living.

Here are some examples from Scripture telling of the importance of being active about our Christian life. The Bible tells us to be sober (which means not being carried away by our emotions) and vigilant (1 Peter 5:8). We are to "run with patience the race that is set before us" (Hebrews 12:1). We are to "fight the good fight of faith" (1 Timothy 6:12). We need to "resist the devil" (James 4:7).

Jesus talked about the need to endure in the context of the increase of evil and the importance of love. He said:

> And because iniquity shall abound, the love of many shall wax cold. But he that shall endure unto the end, the same shall be saved. (Matthew 24:12-13)

This makes it clear that one area which requires us to "endure" is love. No matter what anybody does to us (or to those we love), we need to forgive them, pray for them, and love them. In the face of meanness and nastiness, we need to be patient and kind. Even if we are betrayed, we need to forgive.

THE GREATEST TEXT IN THE BIBLE
By Dr. Harry Ironside (1876-1951)

For God so loved the world, that he gave his only begotten Son, that whosoever believeth in him should not perish, but have everlasting life. (John 3:16)

Why do so many people think this is the greatest text in the Bible? There are other wonderful texts that dwell on the love of God, that show how men are delivered from judgment, that tell us how we may obtain everlasting life, but no other one verse, as far as I can see, gives us all these precious truths so clearly and so distinctly. So true is this that when the Gospel is carried into heathen lands, and missionaries want to give a synopsis of the Gospel to a pagan people, all they find it necessary to do, if they are going to a people who have a written language, is to translate and print this verse, and it tells out the story they are so anxious for the people to hear. If they do not have a written language, invariably one of the first Scriptures they are taught to memorize is John 3:16.

In countries with severe persecution, we see Christians living this way. We can also read about it in *The Hiding Place*, which tells about the experiences of Corrie and Betsy ten Boom in Ravensbruck, a Nazi death camp. You can read about it in the books Corrie wrote after the war when she traveled the world telling people about the love of God and the importance of forgiving. As I mentioned in a previous chapter, there was even a time in her life when one of the cruel guards approached her after she had spoken in a meeting, and she knew she must forgive him, and even love him.

FAITHFUL FRIEND

Lord, you are the friend
who'll never leave me.
You're the friend who'll
always understand.
You will not forsake me or deceive me.
You'll stay by my side until the end.

When I'm afraid, You'll put
Your arm around me.
You're the faithful friend
who's tried and true.
No matter what the troubles
that surround me
You will find a way to get me through.

Your love is strong, it's
deeper than the ocean.
It's higher than the moon
and stars above.
When earth and stars are gone
And time has ended,
I'll still live, rejoicing in Your love.

CHAPTER 12

TAMING THE TONGUE

> For all the law is fulfilled in one word, even in this; Thou shalt love thy neighbour as thyself. But if ye bite and devour one another, take heed that ye be not consumed one of another. This I say then, Walk in the Spirit, and ye shall not fulfil the lust of the flesh. (Galatians 5:14-16)

HOW can people "bite" and "devour" one another? What is the weapon used for that? The mouth. The tongue. Our words.

Remember the old saying, "Sticks and stones can break my bones but words can never hurt me"? Well that is not true. In many cases, words can be more damaging than physical blows. Physical wounds heal much faster and more easily than emotional wounds. The emotional damage can cause problems for a lifetime. I have seen that in the lives of many people I love dearly.

The Bible has some very strong things to say about what we say to one another. We need to be careful not to harm other people by what we say to them. Jesus warned:

> But I say unto you, That whosoever is angry with his brother without a cause shall be in danger of the judgment:

and whosoever shall say to his brother, Raca, shall be in danger of the council: but whosoever shall say, Thou fool, shall be in danger of hell fire. (Matthew 5:22)

But I say unto you, That every idle word that men shall speak, they shall give account thereof in the day of judgment. For by thy words thou shalt be justified, and by thy words thou shalt be condemned. (Matthew 12:36-37)

Paul emphasized the importance of "speaking the truth in love" (Ephesians 4:14-15). He said that our words should "edify" one another (build one another up). We are to avoid "anger" and "evil speaking" and forgive one another. Paul said:

Let no corrupt communication proceed out of your mouth, but that which is good to the use of edifying, that it may minister grace unto the hearers. And grieve not the holy Spirit of God, whereby ye are sealed unto the day of redemption. Let all bitterness, and wrath, and anger, and clamour, and evil speaking, be put away from you, with all malice: And be ye kind one to another, tenderhearted, forgiving one another, even as God for Christ's sake hath forgiven you. (Ephesians 4:29-32)

James said that godly people do not harm others with their words. He said the tongue is small, but it can be destructive like fire. It is "a world of iniquity" and "is set on fire of hell" (James 3:2-7). Then James said:

But the tongue can no man tame; it is an unruly evil, full of deadly poison. Therewith bless we God, even the Father; and therewith curse we men, which are made after the similitude of God. Out of the same mouth proceedeth blessing and cursing. My brethren, these things ought not so to be. (James 3:9-10)

Although no man can tame the tongue, it doesn't depend on our ability. God is able to tame our tongues. When we surrender our lives to Him, He changes our hearts and gives us the grace to overcome our bad habits of the flesh.

Remember the old saying, "Loose lips sink ships"? Well, they can also ruin lives. They can harm other people, and they can also harm our relationship with God. And if those other people are fellow Christians, then God counts it as if we had done that (or said that) to Jesus Himself:

> And the King shall answer and say unto them, Verily I say unto you, Inasmuch as ye have done it unto one of the least of these my brethren, ye have done it unto me. (Matthew 25:40)

That also applies to self-condemnation because we belong to Jesus, and we are His brothers and sisters. There have been times when I've made a foolish mistake and I say to myself (in an angry tone), "You idiot!" And then I've had to repent for doing that because I just said "Thou fool" to someone (namely me) who is a sister of Jesus. I'm one of His brethren, so that applies to me as well.

These Scripture passages about the tongue are challenging and convicting. On the one hand, we need to take what we say very seriously because it impacts the lives of others and it affects our relationship with God. On the other hand, we need to remember that nothing is impossible with God. He can change our hearts so that we don't want to say hurtful things any more.

When it comes to this, and every other aspect of Christian life, we are never going to get it completely right this side of Heaven. The point is, what direction are we moving in?

When Paul called himself "the chief of sinners" (1 Timothy 1:15), I don't think it was just because he used to persecute Christians. I think it was for many other reasons. The closer Paul got to God, the more he became aware of his own sinfulness. We see something similar when Isaiah had that vision/encounter with God:

> Then said I, Woe is me! for I am undone; because I am a man of unclean lips, and I dwell in the midst of a people of unclean lips: for mine eyes have seen the King, the Lord of hosts. (Isaiah 6:5)

Compared to the people of his day, Isaiah was a very righteous man. However, compared to God, he was filthy.

Notice he talked about "unclean lips." He became aware of how he had spoken wrongly to people. After all, Isaiah wasn't just a prophet. He was also a husband and a father, and even the best among us sometimes hurt the people who are closest to us. They are the ones who get hurt when we become exhausted, or overwhelmed, or frustrated by others. It is all too easy to come home and "kick the dog" (i.e., say hurtful things to the spouse or kids).

> But we are all as an unclean thing, and all our righteousnesses are as filthy rags; and we all do fade as a leaf; and our iniquities, like the wind, have taken us away. (Isaiah 64:6)

All of us need to tame our tongues. That includes great men of God like the prophet Isaiah. Once he was in the presence of Almighty God in His holiness, Isaiah suddenly became acutely aware of that.

> Purge me with hyssop, and I shall be clean: wash me, and I shall be whiter than snow. (Psalm 51:7)

Are we willing to change? Are we asking God to enable us to change? Are we repenting when we fail and trying to do better the next time? If we hurt somebody, do we ask them to forgive us? Do we try to undo any damage we have done?

Down here on planet Earth, we are all clumsy children. Every one of us is a mess in one way or another. With some people, it is more visible than with others. And in some cases, it is more extreme. But we are all a mess. That is because, ever since Adam and Eve rebelled against God in the Garden of Eden, our default setting is to sin.

By the grace of God, we can overcome that. But it takes time. It is a process. And it will not be complete until we see the Lord Jesus Christ face to face.

In the meantime, we need to be patient with others and also with ourselves. We need to be merciful to others and also to ourselves. After all, God is patient and merciful.

Behold, we count them happy which endure. Ye have heard of the patience of Job, and have seen the end of the Lord; that the Lord is very pitiful, and of tender mercy. (James 5:11)

---◆——CHAPTER 13——◆——

RESISTING THE DEVIL

> For we wrestle not against flesh and blood, but against
> principalities, against powers, against the rulers of the
> darkness of this world, against spiritual wickedness in
> high places. (Ephesians 6:12)

ANY sin in our lives gives the devil a beachhead from which
to attack us. And it isn't just the specific damage caused by
that particular sin. It is because when we sin, that part of our lives
is in agreement with the devil and opposed to God. In contrast,
look at what Jesus said:

> Hereafter I will not talk much with you: for the prince of
> this world cometh, and hath nothing in me. (John 14:30)

Now we won't get to that point this side of Heaven, but the
closer we can get to it, the better it will be for us and for the people
whose lives we influence.

The basic foundation for being able to resist the devil is sub-
mitting to God. If we are not submitted to God, then we cannot

resist the devil. And to the degree we fail to submit to God, we become more vulnerable to the attacks of the devil. James makes this very clear:

> But he giveth more grace. Wherefore he saith, *God resisteth the proud, but giveth grace unto the humble. Submit* yourselves therefore to God. *Resist* the devil, and he will flee from you. Draw nigh to God, and he will draw nigh to you. Cleanse your hands, ye sinners; and purify your hearts, ye double minded. (James 4:6-8, emphasis added)

Notice the importance of humility here. God resists the proud, but He gives grace to the humble. Therefore, we cannot afford pride. The moment we think we can do things on our own without God is precisely when we are most likely to fall flat on our faces. And as the verse above says, that is when God starts resisting us instead of giving us the grace we need to overcome sin.

Also notice that James talks about being "double minded." According to my father, the Greek term means having two souls. That is two ways of thinking, feeling, and desiring. One part of us wants things God's way with godly thoughts and desires. And another part of us wants things our own way, instead of God's way. And isn't that what caused Lucifer to fall and become the devil instead of being a worshiper in Heaven? He wanted to be like God (i.e., have things his way instead of trusting God and doing things God's way).

Create in me a clean heart, O God;
and renew a right spirit within me.

Cast me not away from thy presence;
and take not thy holy spirit from me.

Restore unto me the joy of thy salvation;
and uphold me with thy free
spirit. (Psalm 51:10-12)

CHAPTER 14

A CLEAN HEART

The heart is deceitful above all things, and desperately wicked: who can know it? (Jeremiah 17:9)

We don't know our own hearts. Or rather, we know them partially. Once Jesus Christ becomes our Lord and Savior, then our hearts are in much better shape, and we know them better. However, we still need to have God show us what is in there that needs to be changed.

Therefore, it is spiritually healthy to develop the habit of inviting God to examine our hearts and make us aware of things that need to be changed. David demonstrates this in the psalms, and we can make his prayers our own as in the following:

> Who can understand his errors? cleanse thou me from secret faults. Keep back thy servant also from presumptuous sins; let them not have dominion over me: then shall I be upright, and I shall be innocent from the great transgression. Let the words of my mouth, and the meditation of my heart, be acceptable in thy sight, O Lord, my strength, and my redeemer. (Psalm 19:12-14)

Nay, in all
these things we
are more than
conquerors
through him
that loved us.
(Romans 8:37)

CHAPTER 15

OVERCOMING OBSTACLES TO TRUSTING THE LORD

How can we increase our trust in God? One way is to identify some of the obstacles to trusting so we can deal with them. We can ask God to: 1) make us aware when we fall into these ways of thinking or reacting; 2) deal with things in our hearts that are fertile ground for these hindrances; and 3) give us practical strategies—and grace—to overcome these problems.

Independence and Self-Reliance

I live in the United States. Our American culture fosters an attitude of independence and self-reliance. It values self-confidence rather than confidence in God. It promotes self-esteem rather than high esteem for God. (We do have great value, but it is not because of any merits of our own. It is because Jesus Christ loves us so much He gave His life in order to save us.)

The American ideal is the self-made man who can say, "I did it!" This promotes the attitude that God warned the Israelites against in Deuteronomy 8:10-18. He warned them not to be deceived into thinking it was *their* power (or education or brilliance or expertise or hard work) that caused them to succeed.

Sometimes, we may have a crisis or danger or an accident or health problems. The result is a "reality check." All at once, we suddenly remember we have to depend on God. That's good. When the crisis is over, we need to keep reminding ourselves of the truth we learned instead of allowing ourselves to slip back into our independent, self-reliant, American mindset.

Our school system indoctrinates us with humanist philosophy and assumptions. Even though we know better as Christians, these things can sneak into our thinking, our assumptions, and our responses. We need to become alert to recognize them and to resist them. The Bible tells us to refuse to allow thoughts to remain if they make it difficult for us to know (and therefore trust) God. The Bible says:

> For though we walk in the flesh, we do not war after the flesh: (For the weapons of our warfare are not carnal, but mighty through God to the pulling down of strong holds;) Casting down imaginations, and every high thing that exalteth itself against the knowledge of God, and bringing into captivity every thought to the obedience of Christ. (2 Corinthians 10:3-5)

The image is a military one, that of a soldier on guard duty who sees someone and says, "Halt! Who goes there?" Then the soldier makes a decision whether to allow the person to stay or require the person to leave; or he may even arrest the person.

Humanism exalts itself against the knowledge of God. It tries to make man the center of the universe and the source of salvation instead of God.

Self-Pity

We live in a culture that encourages people to have a victim mentality. For example, I read a newspaper article about Aristide (the former ruler of Haiti) which said that Aristide was a "victim" of an "addiction to power." A reporter with that kind of attitude could have said the same thing about Adolf Hitler. However, back in Hitler's day, the American public would not have stood for that kind of nonsense.

Some people really have been victimized. I have two friends who were raped when they were young children. They both decided that Jesus is more important to them than what happened to them. And because Jesus told us to forgive, they forgave their rapists. This does not mean that those rapists should not have gone to prison. Innocent people need to be protected from dangerous predators. But the fact that these two women were able to forgive the men who raped them, that turned out to be the key to a process of emotional healing. As they each prayed, read Scripture, and trusted and obeyed the Lord, He healed them by His mercy and grace.

Self-pity is related to humanism. It puts our suffering on center stage instead of God. It says that what happened to us is more important than what Jesus Christ did for us. It says that, because of what happened to us, we don't have to obey Jesus when He tells us to forgive people and to love our enemies. It puts our focus on ourselves instead of on God.

How can we truly trust God when we are focused on ourselves? When we look at ourselves, our problems look huge. When we look at God—and how great and powerful and loving He is—then we can see that, compared to God, our problems are small.

The key to overcoming self-pity is 1) to repent, and 2) to make a decision to focus on who God is and how much He loves us instead of focusing on how we feel.

It is also helpful to get our suffering in perspective. Suffering is a normal part of life. Jesus and the apostles often spoke of it. For example, Jesus said:

> If ye were of the world, the world would love his own: but because ye are not of the world, but I have chosen you out of the world, therefore the world hateth you. Remember

the word that I said unto you, The servant is not greater than his lord. If they have persecuted me, they will also persecute you; if they have kept my saying, they will keep yours also. But all these things will they do unto you for my name's sake, because they know not him that sent me. (John 15:19-21)

The apostle Paul said:

And not only so, but we glory in tribulations also: knowing that tribulation worketh patience; And patience, experience; and experience, hope: And hope maketh not ashamed; because the love of God is shed abroad in our hearts by the Holy Ghost which is given unto us. (Romans 5:3-5)

It is a faithful saying: For if we be dead with him, we shall also live with him: If we suffer, we shall also reign with him: if we deny him, he also will deny us: If we believe not, yet he abideth faithful: he cannot deny himself. (2 Timothy 2:11-13)

Thou therefore endure hardness [hardship], as a good soldier of Jesus Christ. (2 Timothy 2:3)

And being fully persuaded that, what he had promised, he was able also to perform. (Romans 4:21)

The Book of Acts says that Paul and his companions were:

Confirming [strengthening] the souls of the disciples, and exhorting them to continue in the faith, and that *we must through much tribulation enter into the kingdom of God.* (Acts 14:22, emphasis added)

The apostle Peter said:

> Beloved, think it not strange concerning the fiery trial which
> is to try you, as though some strange thing happened unto
> you: But rejoice, inasmuch as ye are partakers of Christ's
> sufferings; that, when his glory shall be revealed, ye may be
> glad also with exceeding joy. (1 Peter 4:12-13)

> Wherein ye greatly rejoice, though now for a season, if
> need be, ye are in heaviness through manifold temptations:
> That the trial of your faith, being much more precious
> than of gold that perisheth, though it be tried with fire,
> might be found unto praise and honour and glory at the
> appearing of Jesus Christ. (1 Peter 1:6-7)

The apostle James said:

> My brethren, count it all joy when ye fall into divers
> temptations; Knowing this, that the trying of your faith
> worketh patience. But let patience have her perfect
> work, that ye may be perfect and entire, wanting
> nothing. (James 1:2-4)

We need to learn to see suffering through the perspective of the
Bible instead of the perspective of our humanist "I have a right to
feel good" culture. Then, no matter what we have been through,
we will be able to get over it and go on with God. We need to be
like the apostle Paul, who said:

> Brethren, I count not myself to have apprehended: but
> this one thing I do, *forgetting those things which are behind,
> and reaching forth unto those things which are before,* I press
> toward the mark for the prize of the high calling of God
> in Christ Jesus. (Philippians 3:13-14, emphasis added)

forgetting those things

which are behind, and

reaching forth unto those

things which are before

Circumstances

Another hindrance to trusting God is believing (or feeling) that our circumstances are so overwhelming that even God can't deal with them in a way that will work out for our good. This is actually a form of idolatry. It is saying that our circumstances are more powerful than God is.

Western culture is saturated with the assumptions of behavioral psychology. This is a humanistic teaching that denies personal responsibility for our own behavior. It says we are at the mercy of our circumstances—that what we do is determined by our present circumstances or by what has happened to us in the past.

This attitude is demonstrated in the movie *West Side Story*. A gang member says, "I'm depraved on account of I'm deprived."

The fatal error of behavioral psychology is thinking that circumstances force people to do things. But circumstances don't have that kind of power. All they can do is pressure people into making personal decisions.

If people take the path of least resistance, then they will go in the direction that the behavioral psychologists predict. However, people are capable of making godly or moral decisions, no matter what the circumstances. God has put something within each person called a conscience. We know right from wrong, even as very young children.

People are swimmers—not driftwood. Floating wood follows wherever the current leads. But a swimmer with a goal will swim towards that goal in spite of the pull of the current.

I knew a young man who was raised in a home where the family was violent and morally depraved. He had no decent role models; he couldn't read, and he didn't know anything about God. But he used to watch a TV program called *Father Knows Best*. As a child, he decided he wanted to be like the people on that TV show instead of being like the people in his family. When he grew up, he met some Christians, heard the Gospel, and became a Christian.

The martyrs demonstrate that people can make godly decisions in spite of great adversity. *Foxe's Book of Martyrs* tells of men and woman who went to their deaths praying or singing. They were more focused on God and His people than they were on their impending death. For example, John Huss died singing, and William Tyndale died praying for the people.

The God who gave strength and courage to Huss and Tyndale will do the same for us when we need it.

During World War II, in Holland, many of the Dutch citizens began to resist the Nazi regime when they realized that Jewish people were being persecuted and murdered. Getting caught helping to hide Jews meant either prison or death. Diet Eman was just nineteen at the time. She and several of her young friends became part of the Christian resistance movement in Holland. They helped save the lives of many Jews, but it cost the lives of most of Diet's friends, including her fiancé. But it was a choice they each made; they did what was right, and they trusted the Lord for the outcome. Of this time period, Diet states:

Sometimes people ask me whether I wish I could skip that whole part of my life, if I could live my life over. I tell them I do not. That part of my life was very, very difficult; I cannot think about it today without crying, even though I never cried much at all for most of that time. But I tell people those years of my life were very special, a time when I was very close to God—so close, in fact, I not only *knew* that He kept His promises, I actually *experienced* His faithfulness.[5]

We can trust God—no matter what happens. If we are faced with grief or tragedy or sickness or injustice or war or persecution, we can trust God to be with us and to get us through it. The apostle Paul said:

Now thanks be unto God, which always causeth us to triumph in Christ, and maketh manifest the savour of his knowledge by us in every place. (2 Corinthians 2:14)

And Jesus said:

I am with you alway, even unto the end of the world. (Matthew 28:20)

The epistle to the Hebrews says:

[F]or he hath said, I will never leave thee, nor forsake thee. So that we may boldly say, The Lord is my helper, and I will not fear what man shall do unto me. (Hebrews 13:5-6)

Again, the apostle Paul said:

And being fully persuaded that, what he had promised, he was able also to perform. (Romans 4:21)

But thanks be to God, which giveth us the victory through our Lord Jesus Christ. (1 Corinthians 15:57)

We are troubled on every side, yet not distressed; we are perplexed, but not in despair; Persecuted, but not forsaken; cast down, but not destroyed. (2 Corinthians 4:8-9)

Not Forgiving

Not forgiving is another ostacle to trusting the Lord. If we don't forgive people, then our relationship with God will be hindered. As a result, it will be more difficult for us to trust God. In addition, lack of forgiveness can have other harmful results in our lives. Forgiveness is such an important subject that I will develop it more in the next chapter.

What Are We Thinking About?

When you drive on a country road with ditches, you have to avoid going off the road on both sides. Whether you go too far to the right or to the left, either way, you will wind up in a ditch.

Some things in the Bible come in pairs. One statement helps us avoid the ditch on one side of the road, and the other statement helps us avoid the ditch on the opposite side.

When it comes to what we think about, we need to understand both sets of principles. On the one hand, we need to have enough understanding of evil to be able to deal with it. On the other hand, we need to focus on good things—not bad ones. You can see both of these principles in Scripture.

Behold, I send you forth as sheep in the midst of wolves: be ye therefore wise as serpents, and harmless as doves. (Matthew 10:16)

Lest Satan should get an advantage of us: for we are not ignorant of his devices. (2 Corinthians 2:11)

Finally, brethren, whatsoever things are true, whatsoever things are honest, whatsoever things are just, whatsoever things are pure, whatsoever things are lovely, whatsoever things are of good report; if there be any virtue, and if there be any praise, think on these things. (Philippians 4:8)

So we need to have enough understanding of bad things to be able to avoid getting snared by them, but at the same time we cannot afford to focus just on such things. We need to focus on good things (and especially on God and His Word). How can we do that in real life?

We do something similar all the time when we drive. We keep our eyes on the road ahead. But at the same time, we are aware of things to the side of the road, such as a deer or another vehicle that could be a potential driving hazard. Our primary focus is straight ahead (which keeps us safe on the road). However, our peripheral vision takes in other things (so we are aware of what is going on around us).

Too Much Focus on Ourselves

The apostle Paul warned about a future time when people would be "lovers of themselves." This would result in a long list of bad attitudes and destructive behavior. Take a look at this list and see how many of these things you can see in our society today:

This know also, that in the last days perilous times shall come. *For men shall be lovers of their own selves,* covetous, boasters, proud, blasphemers, disobedient to parents, unthankful, unholy, Without natural affection, trucebreakers, false accusers, incontinent, fierce, despisers of those that are good, Traitors, heady, highminded, lovers of pleasures more than lovers of God; Having a form of godliness, but denying the power thereof: from such turn away. (2 Timothy 3:1-5, emphasis added)

One form this self-focus takes is the emphasis on "self-esteem." According to Scripture, we are valuable, but the reason is based on God—not on ourselves. We are created in God's image, and Jesus Christ purchased us by His blood. This is what gives us value—not anything we can boast of having said or done. Here is what the Bible says about our own natural goodness, apart from the grace of God:

And he [Jesus] said unto him, Why callest thou me good? there is none good but one, that is, God. (Matthew 19:17)

The heart is deceitful above all things, And desperately wicked: who can know it? (Jeremiah 17:9)

But God hath chosen the foolish things of the world to confound the wise; and God hath chosen the weak things of the world to confound the things which are mighty; And base things of the world, and things which are despised, hath God chosen, yea, and things which are not, to bring to nought things that are: That no flesh should glory in his presence. (1 Corinthians 1:27-29)

Another form that focusing on ourselves takes is self-condemnation. This is more subtle. Because it is a negative perspective imposed on oneself, people can overlook the fact that it is another way of focusing on ourselves instead of focusing on God.

If we have repented of our sins, and God has forgiven them, then why are we still beating ourselves up about it? According to the Bible, the devil is "the accuser" of Christians (Revelation 12:10). Why should we do the devil's job for him?

There is therefore now no condemnation to them which are in Christ Jesus, who walk not after the flesh, but after the Spirit. For the law of the Spirit of life in Christ Jesus hath made me free from the law of sin and death. (Romans 8:1-2)

The Bible tells us to avoid saying destructive things. It says our words should "edify" people. That means to build them up, as opposed to tearing them down.

Let no corrupt communication proceed out of your mouth, but *that which is good to the use of edifying*, that it may *minister grace unto the hearers*. (Ephesians 4:29, emphasis added)

That includes what we tell ourselves. When we talk to ourselves, we are both the speaker and the hearer.

As Christians, we should focus on the Lord and on loving and serving our neighbors. Self-condemnation undermines both of these. It gets our focus on ourselves and makes us the center of attention. It is actually a form of injured pride because it forgets that our value is in Christ alone.

We need to focus on God rather than on ourselves. We should try to see people (including ourselves) the way God sees them and try to live according to biblical principles. The Epistles can be helpful for doing this. They are pastoral letters written to Christians, and they deal with the practical issues of everyday life.

God's Power and Faithfulness

We live in a world that is morally sliding downhill. But we can be reassured because where sin abounds, God's grace abounds even more (Romans 5:20).

If we feel weak or inadequate, then we can be strengthened and comforted by the fact that God told Paul:

My grace is sufficient for thee: for my strength is made perfect in weakness. (2 Corinthians 12:9)

God doesn't play favorites. What He did for Paul, He will do for all of His children. We can rest assured that God's grace really is sufficient for us. When we are weak, He will give us His strength to go on. We can see this same promise in the Epistle of Jude, which says:

Now unto him that is able to keep you from falling, and to present you faultless before the presence of his glory with exceeding joy, To the only wise God our Saviour, be glory and majesty, dominion and power, both now and ever. Amen. (Jude 24-25)

God has provided everything we need in order to overcome every obstacle to trusting Him. The apostle Peter told us:

According as his divine power hath given unto us all things that pertain unto life and godliness, through the knowledge of him that hath called us to glory and virtue: Whereby are given unto us exceeding great and precious promises: that by these ye might be partakers of the divine nature, having escaped the corruption that is in the world through lust. (2 Peter 1:3-4, emphasis added)

We can begin appropriating these "great and precious promises" right now. And then we can spend the rest of our lives learning how to live by them more and more consistently. It's a process and an adventure. We can spend a lifetime doing it here on Earth and then enjoy the fruits of it for all eternity.

And be ye kind
one to another,
tenderhearted,
forgiving one
another, even as
God for Christ's
sake hath
forgiven you.
(Ephesians 4:32)

CHAPTER 16

FORGIVING

ANGER can be dangerous. God knows we can't help getting angry sometimes. However, He warns us that if we let that anger stay with us and take root in us, then we will give the devil an opportunity to harm us. The Bible warns us:

> Be ye angry, and sin not: let not the sun go down upon your wrath: Neither give place to the devil. (Ephesians 4:26-27)

According to *Strong's Concordance*, the word "place" means a condition, a position, or an opportunity. I have a friend whose husband often beat her severely. One day he deliberately threw her down a flight of stairs and broke her back. She had to leave him in order to protect her life and the lives of her children. But she also had to forgive him.

Forgiving him did not mean allowing him to keep on abusing her. It meant not staying angry and not carrying a grudge. The Bible says:

Thou shalt not avenge, nor bear any grudge against the children of thy people, but thou shalt love thy neighbour as thyself: I am the LORD. (Leviticus 19:18)

It also meant having the attitude of Stephen in the Book of Acts. While he was being stoned to death, he prayed for his persecutors, saying:

Lord, lay not this sin to their charge. (Acts 7:60)

God will deal with the people who hurt us. He is both just and loving, and only He really knows their hearts. If we try to avenge it, then it will damage us spiritually and emotionally. It may also harm us physically because long-term anger can cause health problems. And the Bible tells us that God will avenge us when that is necessary:

And shall not God avenge his own elect, which cry day and night unto him, though he bear long with them? (Luke 18:7)

When God tells us to forgive, He is not telling us to be a doormat. Rather, He is saying, "Don't put your hands on the hot stove. Let Me take care of it."

Matthew 18:23-35 is a parable that Jesus taught about a servant who owed his master so much money he could not possibly repay him. His master was compassionate, and he canceled the servant's debt. Then that servant found a fellow servant who owed him a little money and had him thrown into debtor's prison because he was unable to pay him. When the master found out about it, he ordered that the servant who owed him money be turned over to the torturers until he paid the entire debt. Jesus warned:

So likewise shall my heavenly Father do also unto you, if ye from your hearts forgive not every one his brother their trespasses. (Matthew 18:35)

What does being turned over to the torturers mean? And how does that apply to Christians? I really don't know. But whatever it is, I sure don't want to experience it. Forgiving people is a small price to pay to avoid being tormented.

If you know anybody who is eaten up with bitterness, you have probably seen some of that torment. Everything reminds them of the person they are angry at. Their whole life is focused on their grievances. They have stress-related health problems. Their anger spills over onto their families and causes relationship problems. In their anger, they do things that emotionally damage other people, which may tempt those people to become bitter. No wonder the Bible warns us:

Follow peace with all men, and holiness, without which no man shall see the Lord: Looking diligently lest any man fail of the grace of God; lest any root of bitterness springing up trouble you, and thereby many be defiled. (Hebrews 12:14-15)

Why We Should Forgive

It is vital that we forgive, not primarily for the sake of the other person but for our own sake. We don't do it because they deserve to be forgiven. They don't deserve it. But neither do we. And God forgave us in spite of that. Therefore, we should be willing to do the same thing for other people—out of love for God and gratitude for His forgiveness.

Lack of forgiveness can result in long-term anger. And that can have serious consequences. The apostle Paul called it a "work of the flesh" and warned us:

> Now the works of the flesh are manifest, which are these; Adultery, fornication, uncleanness, lasciviousness, Idolatry, witchcraft, *hatred, variance* [contentions], emulations [jealousies], *wrath, strife,* seditions, heresies, Envyings, murders, drunkenness, revellings, and such like: of the which I tell you before, as I have also told you in time past, that they which do such things shall not inherit the kingdom of God. (Galatians 5:19-21, emphasis added)

Note that "wrath" and "strife" are listed right along with sins like murder and adultery. These fruits of unforgiveness can have serious consequences in our lives and in the lives of people who are close to us.

Paul contrasts them with the "fruit of the Spirit," which should characterize our lives as Christians. He said:

> But the fruit of the Spirit is love, joy, peace, longsuffering, gentleness, goodness, faith, Meekness, temperance: against such there is no law. And they that are Christ's have crucified the flesh with the affections and lusts. If we live in the Spirit, let us also walk in the Spirit. (Galatians 5:22-25)

If we want to live biblically and "walk in the Spirit," then God will give us the grace and the strength to do it. This is a process that takes time, patience, and perseverance. We can spend our lives learning to do it more and more consistently. And then we will enjoy the fruit of our labor for all eternity.

To forgive can be difficult. However, when something is clearly necessary, then we do it, no matter how difficult it is. People who have cancer endure painful and difficult treatments in order to get rid of it. Well, bitterness is a kind of emotional and spiritual cancer. No matter how difficult it is, we have to do whatever it takes to get rid of bitterness.

I have learned that one way to forgive someone when it is very difficult to do is to pray for that person in earnestness. It is very hard to remain angry at someone and feel unforgiving toward them when you are praying to the Lord on their behalf. And remember, part of what forgiveness means is giving the hurt and the pain from the trespass against us over to the Lord, allowing Him to carry a burden He has instructed us not to carry.

I once had to forgive someone who had hurt me deeply and betrayed my trust so badly that when I thought about this person, I became physically ill. For over two years, I kept telling God, "You told me to forgive. I want to obey You, but I can't do it. Please change my heart and make me able to forgive."

Then one day I unexpectedly ran into that person. And it was all right. There was no trauma, no stress. In fact, I saw the pain and confusion in this person, and I prayed. God, in His kind mercy, enabled me to love the person who had hurt me so deeply. But I had to persist in continuing to ask God to do it. And I had to cooperate with God's work in my life.

The person who had hurt me so badly did not realize the degree of damage I had endured. This is often the case. As Jesus said:

> Father, forgive them; for they know not what they do.
> (Luke 23:34)

Booker T. Washington was born a slave in 1856. He experienced a lot of injustice, but did he allow it to make him bitter? No. He said, "I let no man drag me down so low as to make me hate him."[6]

When people do things that rightly anger us, we need to forgive the people, give the situation to God, let God take care of it, and get on with our lives. God is more than able to take care of the people and situations that caused us problems.

In addition, when we are wronged, we share in the fellowship of Christ's sufferings. The apostle Paul said:

> That I may know him, and the power of his resurrection, and the fellowship of his sufferings. (Philippians 3:10)

People who go through similar kinds of suffering develop bonds of love and understanding that cannot be built any other way. Being a widow enables me to comfort and encourage other people who have been bereaved. I know what they are going through because I've lived through it myself. A Scripture I quoted earlier is when the apostle Paul said:

> Blessed be God, even the Father of our Lord Jesus Christ, the Father of mercies, and the God of all comfort; Who comforteth us in all our tribulation, that we may be able to comfort them which are in any trouble, by the comfort wherewith we ourselves are comforted of God. For as the sufferings of Christ abound in us, so our consolation also aboundeth by Christ. (2 Corinthians 1:3-5)

Nobody had to forgive people more than Jesus did. When He ministered God's love and compassion, the religious leaders of his day said he was of the devil (Matthew 12:24), and they hated him so much, they plotted to kill him (John 5:18, 7:1).

When we have been wronged and need to forgive people, we are sharing in the fellowship of Christ's sufferings. It gives us a greater appreciation of what Jesus went through for us. We know Him better, and we love Him more. It's worth the price. What it costs us to forgive is a small thing compared to the revelation it gives us of Jesus' love for us.

Anita Dittman was a teenager in Germany during World War II. She was Jewish and also a Christian believer. During Hitler's reign, she saw many horrors. When she was in a work camp, some of the prisoners had a unique opportunity one Christmas Eve to hold a small service. Anita recalls something one of her young friends said to her that snowy night in a Nazi concentration camp:

> The birth of Jesus must have been like this . . . He was poor and persecuted, and He was misunderstood and

STRENGTH FOR TOUGH TIMES

rejected, yet He always forgave. We have to forgive too, Anita, even the Nazis.[7]

This kind of forgiveness cannot be done without the Lord's help. But He promises to help us do what is right.

If you want to see forgiveness in action in modern times, read the Ravensbruck Prayer.

In April 1945, Russian soldiers liberated the Nazi concentration camp at Ravensbruck, Germany. They found the following prayer written on a piece of paper that was wrapped around a stone:

The Ravensbruck Prayer

O Lord, remember not only the men
and women of good will but also those
of ill will. But do not only remember
the suffering they have inflicted on us.
Remember the fruits we bear, thanks
to this suffering—our comradeship,
loyalty, humility, courage, generosity,
and the greatness of heart that has
grown out of all this. And when they
come to judgment, let all the fruits that
we have borne be their forgiveness.

Forgiving Their Captors

The following is an excerpt from *Foxe's Book of Martyrs*. This story took place in the Netherlands in 1568:

[T]hree persons were apprehended in Antwerp, named Scoblant, Hues, and Coomans. During their confinement, they behaved with great fortitude and cheerfulness, confessing that the hand of God appeared in what had befallen them and bowing down before the throne of his providence. In an epistle to some worthy Protestants, they expressed themselves in the following words:

"Since it is the will of the Almighty that we should suffer for His name and be persecuted for the sake of His gospel, we patiently submit and are joyful upon the occasion. We are not comfortless in confinement, for we have faith; we fear not affliction, for we have hope; and we forgive our enemies, for we have charity. Be not under apprehensions for us, we are happy in confinement through the promises of God, glory in our bonds, and exult in being thought worthy to suffer for the sake of Christ. We desire not to be released, but to be blessed with fortitude; we ask not liberty, but the power of perseverance; and wish for no change in our condition, but that which places a crown of martyrdom upon our heads."[8]

Later, each of these men died, but they had forgiven their captors.

Women at work camp during WW II

United States Holocaust Memorial Museum

I call heaven and
earth to record this
day against you, that
I have set before
you life and death,
blessing and cursing:
therefore choose life,
that both thou and
thy seed may live:
(Deuteronomy 30:19)

CHAPTER 17

TAKING GOD SERIOUSLY

In chapter 15, I alluded to the need for balanced thinking in the Christian life by likening it to driving down a country road with ditches on both sides. In other words, while our goal is to stay solidly on the road, we may end up in a "ditch" if we focus on just one aspect of something that takes a balanced approach. The subject of justice and mercy is just such a case.

When it comes to God, some people in the past emphasized sin, Hell, and God's judgment so heavily they forgot about God's love. That is one ditch.

Today, many churches have fallen into the other ditch. They talk about God's love all the time but have forgotten that God is also their Judge. They take sin lightly instead of recognizing how deadly it is. And many people who call themselves Christians these days don't even believe Hell really exists.

Hell is very real. If it wasn't, then why did Jesus die in order to enable us to avoid Hell and go to Heaven? And why did Jesus talk about Hell so often in the Bible?

Some people who call themselves Christians even believe "there are many ways to Heaven"—that Jesus Christ is not the only way. If that were true, then why did Jesus die for us? And why does the Bible so clearly tell us that apart from Jesus, there is no salvation? And if that were true, then that would make Jesus a liar when He said, "I am the way, the truth, and the life: no man cometh unto the Father, but by me" (John 14:6).

In chapters 3 and 4 of the Book of Acts, we see Peter and John heal a lame man who was lying outside of the Temple. Then some of the religious leaders put them in jail for the night and grilled them the next morning. Look at what Peter said to them:

> Then Peter, filled with the Holy Ghost, said unto them, Ye rulers of the people, and elders of Israel, If we this day be examined of the good deed done to the impotent man, by what means he is made whole; Be it known unto you all, and to all the people of Israel, that by the name of Jesus Christ of Nazareth, whom ye crucified, whom God raised from the dead, even by him doth this man stand here before you whole. This is the stone which was set at nought of you builders, which is become the head of the corner. *Neither is there salvation in any other: for there is none other name under heaven given among men, whereby we must be saved.* (Acts 4:8-12; emphasis added)

CHAPTER 18

ROMANS 8:28

And we know that all things work together for good to them that love God, to them who are the called according to his purpose. (Romans 8:28)

As I mentioned in an earlier chapter, years ago my husband had a massive heart attack. He needed a quadruple bypass but was never strong enough to get it. Then he developed congestive heart failure. It took him a year to die, during which time he took so much nitroglycerin for severe chest pains that he called it "pepper candy." During this time, Ray read a lot of Scripture, prayed a lot, and watched Christian TV shows. (This was forty years ago when most of them were good.) Ray grew closer to the Lord, and his love for me grew stronger and deeper.

That was a painful time for both of us, but it was also a good time that bore wonderful fruit in our lives. That pain has long since passed, but in Heaven, Ray and I will both be blessed by the good fruit God brought out of it. That will be part of our "treasure in heaven" (Matthew 6:20).

Years later, I had cancer that required major surgery followed by chemotherapy. I experienced a lot of suffering through this time, but it changed my perspective on life in ways that have continued ever since. It drew me much closer to the Lord, and it made Eternity become much more real to me.

My dad died of cancer. He had major surgery followed by chemotherapy, but the cancer spread to other parts of his body. Mom and Dad both said that going through this was a good experience for them because it brought them closer to God and to one another.

I know people who have had serious health problems, or relationship problems, or financial problems. As a result, they did a lot of praying, and they had to consciously depend on God to get them through every day. These experiences taught them to trust God at a far deeper level. After their situations improved, the level of conscious dependence on God remained, along with a deeper level of trust in Him.

These are a few examples of Romans 8:28. The difficult news is that all of us will face trials and tribulations, pain and hardship, and various kinds of suffering. The good news is God really does work all things out for good for those who truly love Him. According to Scripture, "all things"—there are no exceptions. Jesus said:

> These things I have spoken unto you, that in me ye might have peace. In the world ye shall have tribulation: but be of good cheer; I have overcome the world. (John 16:33)

And Peter wrote in his epistle:

> But the God of all grace, who hath called us unto his eternal glory by Christ Jesus, after that ye have suffered a while, make you perfect, stablish, strengthen, settle you. (1 Peter 5:10)

God Can Bring Good out of Pain and Hardship

In our present, imperfect world, pain and hardship serve a useful and even necessary function. They are like the warning lights on a car, which alert us to things that need attention. This is true physically, mentally, emotionally, and spiritually.

Responsibility for Our Choices

If we ignore "natural laws," we will suffer painful practical consequences. For example, if we touch something hot, we will get burned. If we try to ignore the law of gravity by walking off a roof top, we will fall to the ground and be injured. If we never had to face pain and suffering, we wouldn't have to face the consequences of our actions.

The same is true with spiritual laws. There is a spiritual principle called sowing and reaping. The apostle Paul said:

> Be not deceived; God is not mocked: for whatsoever a man soweth, that shall he also reap. (Galatians 6:7)

If we sow anger, hatred, hostility, bitterness, unforgiveness, ingratitude, selfishness, and the like, we shall receive the same from others. If we choose to cause harm to others, we can expect to receive harm. By the same principle, if we are giving, loving, considerate, thoughtful, and unselfish towards others, we shall receive many blessings. Jesus said:

> Give, and it shall be given unto you; good measure, pressed down, and shaken together, and running over, shall men give into your bosom. For with the same measure that ye mete withal it shall be measured to you again. (Luke 6:38)

This principle does not work perfectly in this life, but it will in Eternity. And even in this imperfect world, those who choose to be giving and loving usually receive love and generosity, while those who choose to give anger and hatred usually receive anger and hatred.

If there were no painful consequences to our negative actions, would we ever learn to give them up? Would we perceive them as harmful and spiritually dangerous if we did not have a pain mechanism to warn us? If there were no unpleasant consequences for violating them, could these even be said to be laws, or would they just be suggestions?

The principle applies more broadly. God has given us certain commandments and laws. For them to be meaningful, there needs to be consequences for violating them and rewards for following them.

In many places, Scripture sets forth blessings and curses. God says, behave in this way and you will be blessed; behave in that way and you will be cursed. For example, in Deuteronomy, chapter 28, God set forth a series of blessings and curses. After describing them in detail for three chapters, God said:

> I call heaven and earth to record this day against you, that I have set before you life and death, blessing and cursing: therefore choose life, that both thou and thy seed may live. (Deuteronomy 30:19)

God uses the possibility of intense suffering as a way of bringing His people into obedience. We see this in the New Testament as well as the Old Testament. The apostle Paul contrasts two ways of life—living by the flesh and living by the Holy Spirit. Living by the flesh results in sexual impurity, idolatry, hatred, discord, jealousy, dissensions, drunkenness, and the like. The results of these are deadly. Paul says:

> [T]hey which do such things shall not inherit the kingdom of God. (Galatians 5:21)

> Let no man deceive you with vain words: for because of these things cometh the wrath of God upon the children of disobedience. (Ephesians 5:6)

In contrast, those who live by the Spirit receive the fruit of the Spirit. This is love, joy, peace, longsuffering, gentleness, goodness, faith, meekness, temperance (see Galatians 5:22-23).

One group is miserable and suffers. The other group is blessed. Paul expresses the difference as that between life and death (Romans 8:5-17).

God has declared that those who believe in Jesus Christ will have eternal life, while those who do not believe in Him are condemned already (John 3:16-18). He has established a judgment in which the righteous (those who are washed in the blood of the lamb) go to "eternal life" and the unrighteous go to "everlasting punishment" (Matthew 25:46). The righteous "will shine forth as the sun in the kingdom of their Father" while the wicked will be thrown into a "furnace of fire" (Matthew 13:42-43, 50; John 5:29).

In all of these, we see the use of pain and suffering as a means of enforcing the laws God has established and as a consequence of violating those laws.

God Can Use Pain and Hardship to Train and Strengthen Us

God's priorities are not the same as ours. We tend to want physical health, freedom from physical and emotional pain, and enough material possessions to live comfortably. We may feel deprived and unjustly treated if we don't have these.

God wants us to have "good" things (Psalm 84:11). However, His primary concern is not with our physical circumstances. His primary concerns are:

- Our eternal salvation
- Our growth into Christian maturity and character
- Our usefulness ("fruitfulness") in the Kingdom of God

The early Christians endured a great deal of suffering. They were a persecuted church. What was their reaction to hardship and suffering? Instead of complaining about it or saying that it was more than they could bear, they welcomed it because it taught them and strengthened them. Look at what James, Peter, and Paul say about it:

> My brethren, count it all joy when ye fall into divers temptations; Knowing this, that the trying of your faith worketh patience. But let patience have her perfect work, that ye may be perfect and entire, wanting nothing. (James 1:2-4)

> [N]ow for a season, if need be, ye are in heaviness through manifold temptations: That the trial of your faith, being much more precious than of gold that perisheth, though it be tried with fire, might be found unto praise and honour and glory at the appearing of Jesus Christ. (1 Peter 1:6-7)

> Now no chastening for the present seemeth to be joyous, but grievous: nevertheless afterward it yieldeth the peaceable fruit of righteousness unto them which are exercised thereby. Wherefore lift up the hands which hang down, and the feeble knees. (Hebrews 12:11-12)

The unanimous voice of the New Testament writers is that pain and suffering teach us, strengthen us, and help us to become mature. These were writers who had experienced considerable suffering in their own lives.

Quite often it seems we grow only in the presence of discomfort or pain that makes us feel the need for change and forces us to cry out to God.

I do want to make one thing clear. These New Testament writers did not seek pain. They never deliberately inflicted it on themselves. But when it came, they took it as an opportunity to grow and learn, knowing that God was still in control of their lives, working everything together for their good.

Some people deliberately inflict pain on themselves as a way of showing devotion to God or attempting to achieve holiness. There is no support for such a view in Scripture. Such behavior is unbiblical and far removed from the attitude of the New Testament writers.

God Uses Hardship and Pain to Get Us to Depend on Him

God can also use hardship, pain, and suffering to get us to depend on Him rather than ourselves. Paul talked about the great pressure he was under in the province of Asia. It was so great that he despaired of life. He said:

> . . . that we should not trust in ourselves, but in God which raiseth the dead. (2 Corinthians 1:9)

Paul asked God to take away his "thorn in the flesh" (2 Corinthians 12:7-8). God replied:

> My grace is sufficient for thee: for my strength is made perfect in weakness. (2 Corinthians 12:9)

How did Paul respond to God's reply? Was he disappointed? Did he fall into self-pity as we so easily do? Not at all. Paul said:

> Therefore I take pleasure in infirmities, in reproaches, in necessities, in persecutions, in distresses for Christ's sake: *for when I am weak, then am I strong.* (2 Corinthians 12:10; emphasis added)

Paul's weakness made him strong in the sense that it caused him to rely to a much greater degree on God's incomparably great strength. God used this "thorn in the flesh" (which evidently bothered Paul quite a bit, whatever it was) to cause Paul to depend on Him at a deeper level.

This is an important biblical principle. We see it illustrated in a number of ways. For example, Jesus said it is hard for a rich man to enter into the Kingdom of Heaven (Matthew 19:23-24). One reason is that a rich person tends to rely on his own riches rather than on God. More generally, those who are comfortably well off and successful by this world's standards often feel they do not need God.

People who are in very difficult situations and do not see how they can get through them are often much more likely to turn to God for help. When life is going well, we can easily believe we are self-sufficient. In the face of hardship and suffering, the delusion of self-sufficiency loses credibility.

We can see this in another way. In the relatively affluent West, the Christian church has tended to be weak. Not only are its numbers declining, but many individuals and churches seem to be lacking in strong commitment to God. Many in the church today will readily compromise convictions that the martyrs would die for in times past.

In other parts of the world, such as Africa, where many people face severe hardships, the Christian church is strong and growing. It is striking that in China, where the independent Christian church faces severe persecution, the church has been growing rapidly. The rate of growth has been far greater under Communist persecution than it ever was before.

Another example is what happened when my dad had to fight the cancer that eventually killed him. Dad said it increased his faith. It put him in a position where he only had God to depend on, and he became willing to depend on God. He identified and got rid of a number of things that had been weakening his faith. He was praying more consistently and more fervently. He gained a greater appreciation and thankfulness for the many blessings that God had given him. And this difficult experience helped him get his knowledge and understanding of God beyond the intellectual head level to a level that reaches the heart.

For my thoughts are not your thoughts,
neither are your ways my ways, saith
the Lord. For as the heavens are higher
than the earth, so are my ways higher
than your ways, and my thoughts
than your thoughts. (Isaiah 55:8-9)

Who shall separate us from the love of
Christ? shall tribulation, or distress, or
persecution, or famine, or nakedness, or
peril, or sword? As it is written, For thy
sake we are killed all the day long; we
are accounted as sheep for the slaughter.
Nay, in all these things we are more than
conquerors through him that loved us.
For I am persuaded, that neither death,
nor life, nor angels, nor principalities, nor
powers, nor things present, nor things to
come, Nor height, nor depth, nor any
other creature, shall be able to separate
us from the love of God, which is in Christ
Jesus our Lord. (Romans 8:35-39)

CHAPTER 19

FACING THE UNEXPECTED

The apostle Paul wrote nearly a fourth of the New Testament. He had amazing revelations about God. Much of our theology is based on his writings. Yet he said:

> For we know in part, and we prophesy in part. (1 Corinthians 13:9)

Paul includes himself among those who only know "in part." If the apostle Paul only knew in part, then no church, no denomination, and no individual has all the answers. All of us have areas where our understanding is limited.

What will we do if things don't make sense to us? Will we become offended with God and abandon our faith? There was a time when many of Jesus' followers became offended with Him and left Him. The apostles were troubled, but they were loyal and remained:

> From that time many of his disciples went back, and walked no more with him. Then said Jesus unto the twelve, Will ye also go away? Then Simon Peter answered him,

Lord, to whom shall we go? thou hast the words of eternal life. (John 6:66-68)

There was a time when King Nebuchadnezzar commanded Shadrach, Meshach, and Abednego to bow down and worship a huge golden idol. If they refused, they would be thrown into a fiery furnace. They answered the king:

> If it be so, our God whom we serve is able to deliver us from the burning fiery furnace, and he will deliver us out of thine hand, O king. But if not, be it known unto thee, O king, that we will not serve thy gods, nor worship the golden image which thou hast set up. (Daniel 3:17-18)

What will we do if the unthinkable happens? Will we be faithful to God no matter what, or will we only be faithful if things work out the way we think they should? The apostle Paul said:

> For the which cause I also suffer these things: nevertheless I am not ashamed: for *I know whom I have believed*, and am persuaded that he is able to keep that which I have committed unto him against that day. (2 Timothy 1:12, emphasis added)

Notice that Paul said "whom" (a person), not "what." Paul's primary confidence was in the person, Jesus Christ. And that is where our primary confidence needs to be. The Bible says:

> Wherefore take unto you the whole armour of God, that ye may be able to withstand in the evil day, and having done all, to stand. (Ephesians 6:13)

This verse says we can expect to have to face at least one "evil day." You may know people who have had to face a number of them.

But even though that time may be incredibly difficult, God will enable us to stand if we cooperate with Him. The apostle Paul said:

> I can do all things through Christ which strengtheneth me. (Philippians 4:13)

According to Jesus, tribulation is a normal part of life. It is to be expected. The important thing is that we can trust Jesus to get us through it. The Bible tells us:

> Trust in the Lord with all thine heart; and lean not unto thine own understanding. In all thy ways acknowledge him, and he shall direct thy paths. Be not wise in thine own eyes; fear the Lord, and depart from evil. (Proverbs 3:5-7)

What if something happens to us which doesn't make sense to us? What if it seems to be contrary to what we were taught by our teachers, or pastor, or our study Bible notes? What will we do?

Will we call God a liar? Or will we say that evidently our teachers didn't fully understand (or adequately explain) that issue? Will we become bitter against God? Or will we choose to trust Him? Will we turn away from God? Or will we turn to Him for strength and comfort and wisdom?

God has promised to make everything work out for our good if we love Him. When the pain and the tears come, will we trust God to bring good out of our situation?

We can ask God to increase our trust in Him and our love for Him. We can ask Him to make us faithful. We can ask Him to enable us to stand with Shadrach, Meshach, and Abednego—to be determined to be faithful to our God no matter what happens to us and the people we love:

> The LORD God is my strength, and he will make my feet like hinds' feet. (Habakkuk 3:19)

ABOUT THE AUTHOR

MY credentials in terms of education or accomplishments aren't impressive. But what I do have is a lifetime of needing God's strength because I've faced many challenges.

As a result, over the years I've paid close attention when preachers or authors or friends shared insights about receiving God's strength and comfort and encouragement. I pondered those things and prayed about them and looked to see whether or not Scripture confirmed them.

Strength for Tough Times was written when I was in need of strength and encouragement myself and therefore reviewed some principles that had helped me in the past. In the process, I realized there are other people who also need strength and encouragement—especially in today's uncertain times. That's why I wrote this book.

When trials come, we can have a wide variety of responses, ranging from "This is terrible!" to being able to "count it all joy" (James 1:2). I'm not yet at the point of being able to "count it all joy." But I'm moving in that direction, and I hope that this book will help you do the same.

When peace,
like a river,
attendeth my way,
When sorrows
like sea billows roll;
Whatever my lot,
Thou has taught me to say,
It is well,
it is well,
with my soul.⁹

ENDNOTES

1. Corrie ten Boom's book *The Hiding Place* tells about how they hid Jews, were sent to a concentration camp, and led a Bible study and prayer meeting there. Some of the prisoners in that camp became Christians through their ministry.

2. Corrie ten Boom, *Clippings from My Notebook* (Nashville, TN: Thomas Nelson Publishers, 1982), p. 27.

3. Josh Turner, "Long Black Train." You can listen to the song on YouTube: www.youtube.com/watch?v=PyRZTAmcW7c.

4. Charles H. Spurgeon, *Morning and Evening: A Con-temporary Version of a Devotional Classic Based on the King James Version* (Peabody, MA: Hendrickson Publishers, Inc., 1991), p. 144.

5. Diet Eman, *Things We Couldn't Say* (Eureka, MT: Lighthouse Trails), p. 325.

6. Booker T. Washington, 1856-1915 (Source unknown; Public Domain).

7. Anita Dittman, *Trapped in Hitler's Hell* (Eureka, MT: Lighthouse Trails Publishing, 3rd edition), p. 134.

8. John Foxe, *Foxes Book of Martyrs* (Public Domain).

9. Horatio Spafford, 1873, *It is Well with my Soul* (Public Domain).

PHOTO AND ILLUSTRATION CREDITS

Title page and page 84: www.bigstockphoto.com; used with permission.

Flowered border for title pages: Alina Pavlova, www.123rf.com; used with permission.

Page 28: Photo of El Capitan from Yosemite National Park, California; bigstockphoto.com; used with permission.

Page 45: www.bigstockphoto.com; used with permission.

Pages 46 and 60: Taken from the *Compendium of Illustrations in the Public Domain* (all art is in the public domain).

Pages 70, 82, 90, 119: www.bigstockphoto.com; used with permission.

Page 107: Photo used from *Trapped in Hitler's Hell*; courtesy United States Holocaust Museum; used with permission.

Page 120: Watercolor painting by Jeannette Dube; used with permission.

OTHER RESOURCES

You may find the following resources helpful in gaining a biblical perspective about challenging situations.

1. *The Hiding Place*. Corrie ten Boom's family hid Jews during World War II. They experienced the worst of human depravity, and the love and faithfulness of God. Corrie's book *The Hiding Place* can help us trust God more and get our own trials in better perspective. There is also a DVD (with the same title) based on the book.

2. *Trapped in Hitler's Hell* by Anita Dittman.

3. *Things We Couldn't Say* by Diet Eman.

4. The Shepherd's Way, www.shepherd.to: the ministry website of Berit Kjos. Hymns and Scriptures to comfort and exhort.

5. And last, but most importantly, read and study the Word of God.

SCRIPTURE-VERSE INDEX

ALSO BY MARIA KNEAS

HOW TO PREPARE FOR HARD TIMES AND PERSECUTION

$13.95 | Softbound | 232 Pages

Available through Lighthouse Trails and most bookstore outlets

Official government documents say that evangelical Christians are potential terrorists, and some Christian groups are even called hate groups. Christian doctors and nurses are being forced to perform abortions, and a Christian baker has been threatened with prison for not baking a wedding cake for a homosexual couple. Christians in Colorado, New York, and Kentucky are being forced to go through "sensitivity training" in order to "rehabilitate" from their religious beliefs and resulting moral convictions. When Communists did such things to American soldiers, we called it brainwashing.

American Christians are in the early stages of persecution, and it is increasing. Unfortunately, many will be blindsided by it because few pastors and church leaders are warning about it or preparing believers for it.

The first part of *How to Prepare for Hard Times and Persecution* is based on years of research into current events looked at from a biblical perspective. It discloses what is happening, how we got there, and where we are heading. The second part gives encouragement from Scripture and biblical principles for dealing with the challenges of the perilous times in which we live. As Christians, we cannot afford to compromise our faith. We need to believe and obey the inspired Word of God. We need to be prepared to respond to persecution biblically instead of reacting to it carnally.

A MUST READ FOR EVERY CONCERNED CHRISTIAN

To order additional copies of:
Strength for Tough Times, 2ⁿᵈ ed.
Send $11.95 per book plus shipping
($2.95 for 1 book, $6.00 flat rate for all other orders) to:

Lighthouse Trails Publishing
P.O. Box 908
Eureka, Montana 59917

For bulk rates of 10 or more copies, contact Lighthouse Trails
Publishing, either by phone, online, e-mail, or fax. You may order
online at www.lighthousetrails.com or
for US & Canada orders, call our toll-free number: 866/876-3910.

For international and all other calls: 406/889-3610
Fax: 406/889-3633

Strength for Tough Times, as well as other books by Lighthouse Trails
Publishing, can be ordered through all major outlet stores, bookstores,
online bookstores, and Christian bookstores. Bookstores may order through:
Ingram, SpringArbor, Anchor, or directly through Lighthouse Trails.

Libraries may order through Baker & Taylor.
Quantity discounts available for most of our books.

For other resources, visit our website at:
www.lighthousetrails.com

Also check out our tea product line:
Shepherd's Organic Bible Verse Tea
"A Bible verse with every tea bag"
www.theshepherdsgarden.com

You may learn more about the author at
www.mariakneas.com and www.lighthousetrails.com.